W9-AZF-716

25 Bicycle Tours
in and around
Washington, D.C.

From the Capitol Steps
to Country Roads

Anne H. Oman

Photographs by Anne H. Oman
and Tabitha R. Oman

A 25 Bicycle Tours™ Book

Backcountry Publications
Countryman Press, Inc.
Woodstock, Vermont

An Invitation to the Reader

Although it is unlikely that the roads you cycle on these tours will change much with time, some road signs, landmarks, and other terms may. If you find that changes have occurred on these routes, please let us know so we may correct them in future editions. Address all correspondence:

Editor
25 Bicycle Tours™ Series
Backcountry Publications
P.O. Box 175
Woodstock, VT 05091

Library of Congress Cataloging-in-Publication Data

Oman, Anne H.
   25 bicycle tours in and around Washington, D.C.: from the capitol steps to country roads/Anne H. Oman; photographs by Anne H. Oman and Tabitha R. Oman.
      p.   cm.
   "A 25 bicycle tours book."
   ISBN 0-88150-190-5:
   1. Bicycle touring—Washington Region—Guide-books. 2. Cycling paths—Washington Region—Guide-books. 3. Washington Region—Description and travel—Guide-books. I. Title. II. Title: Twenty-five bicycle tours in and around Washington.
   GV1045.5.W18043   1991
   796.6'4'09753—dc20   90-26986
                                                                   CIP

© 1991 by Anne H. Oman, Third Printing

All rights reserved. No part of this book may be reproduced in any form or by any electronic or mechanical means, including information storage and retrieval systems without permission in writing from the publisher, except by a reviewer, who may quote brief passages.

Published by Backcountry Publications
A division of The Countryman Press, Inc.
Woodstock, Vermont 05091

Printed in the United States of America by McNaughton & Gunn
Typesetting by The Sant Bani Press
Text and cover design by Richard Widhu
Maps by Richard Widhu, © 1991 Backcountry Publications
Photo on page 83 by Archie Smith, page 71 courtesy Gunston Hall
All others by Anne H. Oman and Tabitha R. Oman
Layout and Paste-up by Anne Davis
Printed on recycled paper

Acknowledgments

I'd like to thank all of the people who went on these tours with me, especially my family, the Gourleys, the Martins, Tato Joelson, Dwayne Poston, and Betsy Agle They endured rain, wrong turns, and other tribulations in the interest of research on this book. I would also like to thank Carl Taylor of Backcountry Publications, who inspired and encouraged me throughout the research and writing period, and Ricia Gordon, who put an eagle eye and an educated pencil to the manuscript.

Publisher's notice: Cycling involves inherent risks, and readers planning to follow tours in this book should first read carefully the "safety" section of the introduction. Cyclists in urban areas should also be alert to the problem of crime. Tours in this book are in areas considered safe to ride in at the time of publication, but cyclists should follow sensible precautions (such as never cycling at night and traveling with one or more companions) and should be alert to changing patterns of crime in the city.

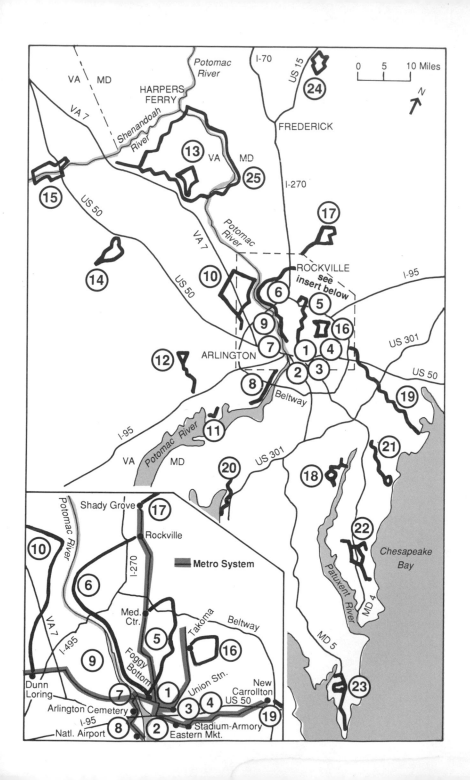

Contents

Cyclists and others browse at a craft fair at the historic Freeman Store, on the Washington and Old Dominion Trail in Vienna, Virginia.

Introduction

Washington is a big, booming metropolis, but a great place to bike. A system of trails, a disproportionate number of national and local parks, a subway system accessible to cyclists at certain times, and a network of activist cyclists who lobby for better bicycling conditions all combine to make the Washington area hospitable to two-wheeled touring. The Washington area also has an amazing variety of natural and built attractions—from the Great Falls of the Potomac to the Washington Cathedral, from the beaches of the Chesapeake Bay to the Civil War town of Harpers Ferry. Seeing these places by bicycle gives them added interest.

About the Rides

The tours in this book are designed to take the rider to well-known and lesser-known places within the city of Washington and its suburbs—and to facilitate getaways to rural areas surprisingly close to the city. The rides will appeal most to people who like to combine cycling with visiting historic and scenic points of interest.

There are rides in this book to suit just about every level of cycling ability and every time frame. A short ride around the National Arboretum or through Arlington Cemetery makes a nice family activity on a Sunday afternoon. The trip to Harpers Ferry is ideal for a three-day weekend. Most of the trips can easily be completed in one day—but some can be stretched into overnight trips if schedules permit. The people who made the trips with me ranged in age from 7 to 50–plus. You can set your own pace on these tours. If you have children or people unused to cycling in your party, you'll want to take more rest stops and allow extra time to walk up some hills.

Because different cyclists set different paces, I haven't tried to estimate the time necessary to complete a tour. You can spend all day on a 10-mile tour if you stop often to rest, picnic, swim, and see the sights. On the other hand, you can easily ride 40 to 50 miles in less than a day. I found 25 miles to be a good distance for a one-day tour—challenging enough but allowing time for poking around old cemeteries or wading in streams. I've tried to avoid backtracking, but sometimes this wasn't possible.

The rides are organized geographically, but, because of the nature of the metropolitan area, the distinctions are not as neat as they might be. Some rides listed under "District of Columbia," for example, might begin in the District and end in Maryland.

Within jurisdictions, the tours that begin closest to downtown Washington are listed first, and those farthest away are listed last.

About the Metro

Many of the tours start from Metrorail stations. Bicyclists are allowed to bring their bikes on the trains evenings after 7 p.m. and on weekends and holidays except July 4 if they have permits. Using the Metro is great because it gets you nearer to your destination, without the bother and expense of car bike racks. It's easy to obtain a permit, but you must appear in person at Metro's main office at 600 Fifth Street NW for a briefing and test on the common-sense bike-on-rail rules. Call 202-962-1116 for more information and for the hours when the permits are issued. If you don't want to use Metrorail, many of the stations have parking lots that are free on weekends. For more information about parking at Metro stations, call 202-637-7000. Where possible, alternative starting places are given.

About Safety

Cycling in a metropolitan area involves two kinds of safety considerations. A cyclist needs to protect himself or herself from criminal activity as well as from traffic hazards. The tours in this book are all in areas considered safe, in daylight hours, at the time of publication. But "safe" is a relative term, and no place is completely without danger. Prudent cyclists will use common sense to protect themselves and their bikes against crime and other dangers. Here are some important safety tips.

- Never ride alone, particularly on a secluded trail or road.
- Always let someone know what route you are taking.
- Don't ride after dark.
- Carry a whistle around your neck or an air horn in an accessible pocket. Noise can both bring help and scare away attackers.
- Ride with the traffic flow. This is a legal requirement.
- Wear a helmet. (See "About Equipment.")
- Use hand signals before turning. A left arm out straight signals a left turn. A left arm bent upward at a right angle signals a right turn. A left arm bent downward at a right angle signals slowing or stopping.
- When riding with companions, ride single file at least 20 feet apart.
- Don't wear headsets or ear plugs.
- Be sure your bicycle is in good working order.

On a knoll overlooking the Potomac River, Mount Vernon, home of the first president, is at the end of a 17-mile bike path.

- Watch out for storm drains, potholes, railroad or trolley tracks, patches of sand or gravel, and other road hazards.
- Ride defensively. Cars are bigger than you are. Watch for people opening the doors of parked cars on your side.
- Pull well away from the road when you stop to rest or check the map.

Bike Security

Always secure your bike when you leave it—even for a few minutes. This is especially important in urban areas, where bicycle theft is a serious problem. The kind of lock most likely to foil would-be bicycle thieves is the U-shaped shackle lock, sold under such brand names as Kryptonite and Citadel. These are expensive—but not as expensive as a new bicycle. And police departments in some jurisdictions report that bicycle thefts have actually declined since these locks were introduced in the 1970s. Here are some basic security guidelines.

• Lock your bike to something permanent and in a place where any attempted theft is likely to be noticed.

• Lock up as much of your bike as possible. If you have quick-release wheels, remove the front wheel and put the lock through the front wheel, the rear wheel, and the frame, securing it to the rack, tree, or other fixture. Remove any accessories you don't want to lose — pumps, water bottles, and computer-type odometers are vulnerable to theft.

• Register your bike with your local police department. This will greatly enhance your chances of getting it back if it's stolen.

About Equipment

All you really need are a touring or mountain bike in good condition, a helmet, a lock (see above), and clothing suitable for the weather. The Washington Area Bicyclist Association (WABA) publishes a Consumer's Guide to Bicycle Helmets. To obtain a copy, call 202-944-8567.

Other useful equipment includes a patch kit and spare tube, a bike-mounted air pump, a bike-mounted water bottle, a rear-view mirror attached either to your helmet or to your handlebars, an odometer (either the computer type that is installed on your handlebars or the less expensive mechanical variety that attaches on your front wheel), and some kind of carrying device. Packs that attach to your bike are more comfortable than backpacks.

Bike Rentals

Many bicycle shops rent bikes, racks, child carriers, helmets, and other equipment. If you want to rent a bike for a particular tour, call the bike shop listed at the end of the tour. In addition, rental bikes are available at Fletcher's Boat House (202-244-0461) on the Chesapeake and Ohio Canal and at Thompson's Boat Center (202-333-4861), convenient to the C & O Canal trail, the Rock Creek trail, and DC monuments.

Sources for Maps and Other Information

Maps in this book are designed to provide all the information bicyclists taking these tours will need. However, you can obtain additional maps and tips from the various political jurisdictions — states, counties, etc. An easier method is to send a self-addressed stamped envelope to the Washington Area Bicyclist Association (WABA) and ask for a list of maps and other guides. WABA will send you an order form and will fill your order promptly. You may also visit the association's shop to purchase your maps: 1015 31st Street NW, Washington DC 20007-4406, 202-944-8567.

Organized Cycling

Several groups in the Washington area run frequent group cycling trips. Foremost among these are:

Potomac Pedalers Touring Club. Each weekend, the Potomac Peddlers run a dozen or more trips for cyclists of varying abilities. The group rates each ride according to 7 categories, which range from "Casual" (from 5 to 15 miles in length), to "Fast Training" (for race-oriented cyclists). Nonmembers are welcome on the rides, but it's difficult to find out about them if you're not a member. The schedule is published in the club newsletter, *Pedal Patter,* which is mailed to members and is also available at some bicycle shops. Each ride has a leader, whose phone number is listed in the newsletter description in case a reader needs more information. There are no charges for the rides. For membership information, call 202-363-TOUR.

American Youth Hostels. This group offers rides most weekends, usually recreational rides to points of interest and suitable for casual cyclists. Most rides include a lunch or snack stop, and the ride fee covers this plus van transportation from the Washington hostel at 11th and K Streets NW. For a recorded message about currently scheduled tours, call 202-783-4944. The recording includes a number to call for further information.

In addition, other groups offer rides on an occasional basis. Check for "Cycling" in the sports listings in Friday's "Weekend" section of the *Washington Post.*

District of Columbia Tours

1.

Museums, Monuments, and other Major Sights

Location: District of Columbia
Terrain: One fairly steep uphill climb, otherwise flat with only a few moderate hills
Road conditions: Bike paths and some city streets with light traffic on weekends
Distance: 10.6 miles
Highlights: Washington's major monuments and museums plus Georgetown, Embassy Row, the White House, etc.

This is a great tour if you're a newcomer to Washington or if you want to show visitors your city from a different perspective. (To find out where you can rent bikes for visitors, see the list of bicycle shops at the end of this chapter.) While it will only take a couple of hours to breeze by all these attractions, you can easily spend all day on this tour if you actually visit the sights. Be sure to bring good bike locks.

Start your tour at Union Station, either at the Metro stop or in the parking lot. Be sure to take time either before or after the tour to explore the station building, which is loosely modeled on Rome's Baths of Caracalla. Still in use as a major train station, it also holds shops, restaurants, food stands, and nine movie theaters.

0.0 Cross Massachusetts Avenue in the pedestrian crosswalk in front of the Christopher Columbus fountain. Turn left; then take a right onto First Street NE. Ride up the hill, between the Russell and Dirksen Senate Office Buildings and past the Supreme Court.

0.5 Turn right onto the grounds of the U.S. Capitol.

Park your bike in the rack on the north side of the building and enter by climbing the steps in the center of the east side. You'll then be in the Rotunda, under the cast-iron dome, where tours begin all day,

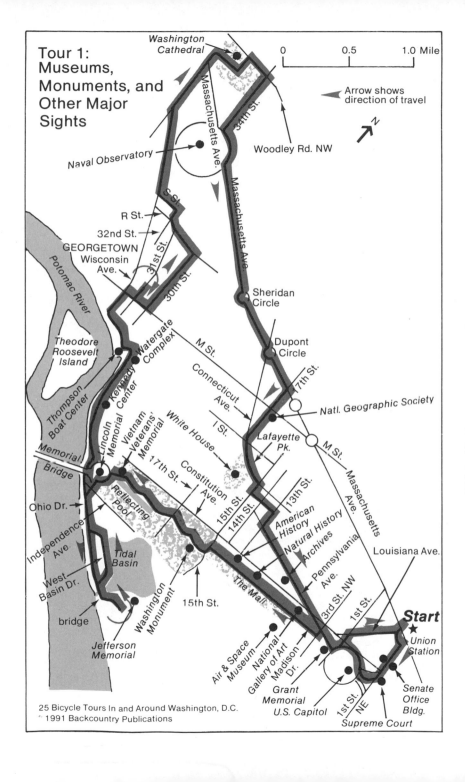

Tour 1:
Museums, Monuments, and Other Major Sights

0   0.5   1.0 Mile

Arrow shows direction of travel

N

Washington Cathedral

Massachusetts Ave.

34th St.

Woodley Rd. NW

Naval Observatory

S St.

R St.

32nd St.

GEORGETOWN
Wisconsin Ave.

31st St.

30th St.

Sheridan Circle

Potomac River

Theodore Roosevelt Island

Thompson Boat Center

Watergate Complex

Kennedy Center

M St.

Dupont Circle

Connecticut Ave.

17th St.

Natl. Geographic Society

Lincoln Memorial

Vietnam Veterans' Memorial

White House

I St.

Lafayette Pk.

M St.

Massachusetts Ave.

Memorial Bridge

17th St.

Constitution Ave.

15th St.

14th St.

13th St.

American History

Natural History

Archives

Louisiana Ave.

Ohio Dr.

Reflecting Pool

Independence Ave.

Tidal Basin

Pennsylvania Ave.

3rd St. NW

1st St.

West Basin Dr.

bridge

Washington Monument

15th St.

The Mall

Start

Union Station

Jefferson Memorial

Air & Space Museum

National Gallery of Art

Madison Dr.

Grant Memorial

U.S. Capitol

1st St. NE

Supreme Court

Senate Office Bldg.

25 Bicycle Tours In and Around Washington, D.C.
© 1991 Backcountry Publications

Begun in 1793 when George Washington laid the cornerstone, the U.S. Capitol was finished under Lincoln, who called its completion "a sign we intend the Union shall go on."

every day between 9 a.m. and 4:30 p.m. After the tour, walk out on the West Terrace for a view of the Mall and the Washington Monument and Lincoln Memorial.

Reclaim your bike and head down Capitol Hill.

0.8 You may want to rest here and admire the Grotto, a sylvan structure designed by Frederick Law Olmstead, who landscaped the Capitol grounds as well as New York's Central Park. The small brick shelter was built around a spring, but the spring turned impure and was replaced by a water fountain.

At the bottom of the hill, cross First Street NW, circling around the Navy Memorial.

0.9 **Stop at the Grant Memorial, one of the capital's most compelling, and bike around the north rim of the Capitol Reflecting Pool.**

Cross Third Street NW and enter Madison Drive, which parallels the Mall on the north side.

1.3 The National Gallery of Art (right) includes the angular I.M. Pei East Wing—which houses Calder mobiles, Joan Miro tapestries, and changing exhibits—and the classical West Wing, home to paintings ranging from the Renaissance to the 20th century. There's a bike rack at the east entrance to the West Wing. Continue along Madison Drive, stopping to visit museums and other attractions at will.

1.4 The National Air Force and Space Museum is on the left across the Mall. The National Archives, repository of the Constitution and the Declaration of Independence, is on your right across Constitution Avenue.

1.5 The National Museum of Natural History (right) houses the Hope diamond, an insect zoo, dinosaur skeletons, and millions of other artifacts. Across the Mall is the Smithsonian "Castle," which holds the tomb of James Smithson. The scholarly illegitimate son of an English lord, Smithson left his fortune to establish in the United States an institution devoted to knowledge, even though he never visited this country. Adjacent to the castle is a carousel.

1.6 Across the Mall is a complex of underground museums devoted to Asian, African, and Pacific Island art. Adjacent to this complex is the above-ground Freer Gallery with a fine collection of Asian art plus representative paintings by Winslow Homer, James Whistler, and others. A highlight is the Peacock dining room designed and decorated by Whistler.

1.7 Park your bike in the rack in front of the National Museum of

American History and browse through the eclectic collection, which includes the inaugural ball gowns of all the first ladies, the red slippers from the movie *The Wizard of Oz,* and the original flag that inspired Francis Scott Key to write "The Star Spangled Banner." The Mall ends here, at 14th Street, but Madison Drive continues one more block to 15th Street.

1.9 **Cross 15th Street in the pedestrian crossing and ride up the hill to the Washington Monument.**

Even if you don't want to wait in line long enough to ascend, you'll have a fine view of the Lincoln Memorial and the Reflecting Pool ahead of you and of the White House to your right.

Take the path that veers off to your right and follow it to the crosswalk across 17th Street.

2.2 **Walk your bike across 17th Street in the crosswalk and enter the wide, hard-packed dirt trail that runs beside the Reflecting Pool.**

The pool was modeled on those leading to the palace at Versailles and to the Taj Mahal.

2.5 **Lock your bike in the rack near the information kiosk and visit the Lincoln Memorial and the Vietnam Veterans Memorial.**

There are rest rooms under the Lincoln Memorial and if you visit them you can also view the stalactites that grow under the monument.

Follow the sidewalk to your left around the memorial and cross Independence Avenue near the Ericson Memorial, dedicated to the inventor of the screw propeller. Cross Ohio Drive and enter the bike path, heading left.

You may want to rest under the willows on the banks of the Potomac and gaze over at Arlington House, home of Robert E. Lee, on the Virginia side.

3.0 The Air Mail Rock (left) marks the take-off point for the first regular air mail service, begun on May 15, 1918, serving Washington, Philadelphia, and New York. In the fields beyond, you can often catch weekend polo matches or rugby games.

3.3 **Follow Ohio Drive as it veers left and cross the Inlet Bridge over the Tidal Basin.**

Observe the fish-tailed gargoyles on the bridge. They were added in 1987 and their faces were copied from a photograph of the then head of the National Park Service, Jack Fish.

As soon as you've crossed the bridge, bear left to the Jefferson Memorial. After visiting the memorial, double back across the bridge and take West Basin Drive to your right. This will lead you past the famous cherry trees, a gift from Japan.

3.9 At the fork, bear left, following the signs toward the Lincoln Memorial. Cross Ohio Drive and reenter the bike path, heading right.

4.2 Pass under Memorial Bridge, where the path narrows. Walk your bike.

> 4.3 The Watergate Steps, which preceded the famous apartment complex by several decades, served as a ceremonial entry to Washington for VIPs arriving by sea. Later, but before airplane and road noise precluded the idea, the steps were the site of concerts. Old movie buffs may remember that Sophia Loren skipped out of a concert here to begin her romance with Cary Grant in *House Boat.*

> 4.9 On your right is the Kennedy Center for the Performing Arts and, just beyond it, the Watergate Complex.

5.1 Turn left to Thompson's Boat Center (bike and boat rentals available); then bear right and walk your bike on the brick sidewalk that leads along the newly renovated Georgetown waterfront.

> You'll pass fountains, outdoor cafes, and a realistic sculpture of a man in a turtleneck and cap filling his pipe. Across the river (left) lies Theodore Roosevelt Island, a nature preserve. You'll probably see crews and individuals rowing on the river.

5.2 Turn right, exit the waterfront complex, and enter Wisconsin Avenue, riding uphill.

5.3 Cross a bridge over the C & O Canal. (See Tour 6.) Continue up Wisconsin to M Street and turn right. Watch for heavy traffic in the heart of the Georgetown commercial area.

5.4 Cross M Street at 31st in the pedestrian crosswalk and walk your bike to the Old Stone House at 3051 M Street NW.

> Built in 1765, the oldest surviving residential structure in the city is open for tours Wednesday through Sunday. It was the home of a cabinetmaker and his family and provides a rare glimpse of what life was like for the middle class in the 18th century. The garden in back is a great place for picnics, and carry-out food is available at several places on M Street. Continue east on M Street to 30th Street; then turn left up 30th Street through the fashionable 19th-century Georgetown residential district.

5.8 Turn left onto R Street, skirting Oak Hill Cemetery and Montrose Park (right).

> At 31st and R Streets is the entrance to Dumbarton Oaks Gardens, containing formal and informal gardens and fountains and an "orangerie." The gardens are open 2 to 6 p.m. daily, and there is an admission charge.

5.9 Turn right onto 32nd Street.

The Dumbarton Oaks Museum, including the house where the postwar treaty was negotiated, the Pre-Columbian collection, and the Byzantine collection, is located at 1703 32nd Street. It's open Tuesday through Sunday from 2 to 5 p.m., and a donation is suggested.

6.0 Turn left onto S Street, then right onto Wisconsin Avenue. Be prepared for heavy traffic and a steep climb.

6.7 On your left is the Soviet Embassy's residential and office complex on a site known as Mount Alto. Before glasnost, a great brouhaha developed when it was discovered that, from this elevated site, the Soviets could intercept secret signals.

6.9 Turn right onto South Road on the Washington Cathedral grounds.
This Gothic cathedral, in the style of 14th-century English ecclesiastical architecture, was begun in 1907 and completed in 1990. Volunteers give tours and point out the moon rock incorporated into a stained glass window, the crypt of Woodrow Wilson (the only President buried in the District of Columbia), and other features. An elevator takes visitors to the Pilgrim Gallery for a spectacular view from one of Washington's highest points.

After visiting the cathedral, take the road to the right of the building, past the peaceful Bishops Garden. Bear left at the nursery and exit the cathedral grounds at Woodley Road NW.

7.1 Turn right on Woodley Road.

7.2 Turn right on 34th Street. Watch for heavy traffic.

7.7 Turn left onto Massachusetts Avenue NW.
As soon as you make the turn, you'll see the U.S. Naval Observatory on your right. You may enter only if you go on one of the 90-minute tours, which are held weekdays at 12:30 and 2 p.m. On the grounds is the Vice President's house, which is not open to the public.

8.0 The British Embassy complex (right) includes a modern office building that was added onto the residence designed by Sir Edward Luytens, architect of many of the great country houses of England. In front of the residence, with one foot on the embassy's British soil and one foot on American soil, is a statue of Winston Churchill, cigar in hand. Across Massachusetts Avenue is the South African Embassy, gathering point for anti-apartheid demonstrations.

8.1 The embassies of Bolivia and Brazil are on the right. Across the avenue is the old Iranian Embassy, which was commandeered by the State Department during the hostage crisis and is now used for State Department functions.

8.2 The Islamic Center and Mosque (left) was built with monetary and material contributions from many Moslem countries. Note that it does not face the street exactly — it faces Mecca. Non-Moslem visitors are welcome. You must remove your shoes before entering.

8.3 The Embassy of Japan is on the right and the Embassy of Venezuela, on the left.

8.5 The United Arab Emirates Embassy is on your right. The limestone chateau across the avenue, designed in 1906 by local architect George Oakley Totten, serves as the Embassy of Cameroon.

8.6 **Yield to traffic in Sheridan Circle, which contains a statue of General Sheridan on his horse, Rienzi.**
The work is nicknamed "an officer and a gentleman." On your right is the Embassy of Turkey.

8.7 Anderson House (right) contains a museum of artifacts of the Society of the Cincinnati, an organization of descendants of George Washington's officers, and a lovely garden. It's open for tours Tuesday through Saturday afternoons.

8.8 The Embassy of Indonesia (right) occupies the former home of Evelyn Walsh McLean, whose father struck it rich in the Colorado gold fields and who owned the Hope diamond.
Continue on Massachusetts Avenue through Dupont Circle.

9.1 **Turn right onto 17th Street NW and continue to the intersection of 17th and M Streets.**
Lock your bike to a tree or sign and visit Explorers Hall of the National Geographic Society. It's open daily and the changing exhibits are free.

9.5 **At I Street, 17th Street intersects with Connecticut Avenue. Bear left on Connecticut to Lafayette Park.**
The square surrounding the park is actually known as Jackson Square, and, although there is a statue of Lafayette in the park, the central place is occupied by an equestrian statue of Andrew Jackson, his horse rearing in the direction of the house he once occupied. Washington's elite — including Henry Adams, John Hay, Dolly Madison, and Stephen Decatur — lived on this square. Many of the houses have been preserved and are used as government offices. The Stephen Decatur House, on the northwest corner of the square, is open to the public. You may also visit St. John's, "the church of Presidents," at the corner of 16th and H Streets.
Walk your bike through the park and cross Pennsylvania Avenue in the crossing in front of the White House. The White

House is open for tours Tuesday through Saturday mornings. Expect a long line. Turn left and follow Pennsylvania Avenue past the Treasury Building.

9.7 Following the inaugural parade route—but backwards—turn right on 15th Street NW. Just past the Treasury Building, cross in the pedestrian crossing into Pershing Square.

The Square contains a memorial to General "Black Jack" Pershing plus an ice-skating rink that turns into a water garden in summer.

Cross 14th Street and enter the Western Plaza, with its fountains and inscriptions about the city. On your right is the Beaux Arts–style District Building, Washington's city hall. Walk or ride across the plaza; then cross Pennsylvania Avenue and continue riding down the "avenue of Presidents."

9.9 The Old Post Office Building, saved from the wrecking ball in the 1970s, holds shops and restaurants. There's a great view from the tower. Across Pennsylvania Avenue is the Hoover Building, F.B.I. headquarters. The popular tours of this building are available weekdays from 8:45 a.m. to 4:15 p.m. Expect to wait in line.

10.0 The Navy Memorial and bandstand (left) was undertaken as part of the Pennsylvania Avenue spruce-up.

10.1 Modern and monumental, the Canadian Embassy (left) is the first embassy to be built on Pennsylvania Avenue. Its gallery features works by Canadian artists and is open to the public.

10.3 Pennsylvania Avenue NW ends at the foot of Capitol Hill. Turn left on First Street NW and follow it past the intersection with Constitution Avenue. Bear right on Louisiana Avenue.

10.6 Return to the starting point, Union Station.

Bicycle Repair Service
Southeast Cycle, 629 Pennsylvania Avenue SE, (202-543-5533)
Big Wheel Bikes, 1034 33rd Street NW, (202-337-0254)
The Bicycle Exchange, 4000 Wisconsin Avenue NW, (202-244-2800)
The Bike Shop at District Hardware, 2003 P Street NW, (202-659-8686).

2.

Wandering Washington's Waterfront

Location: The District of Columbia
Terrain: Flat
Road conditions: Paved bike trails, park roads, and city streets
Distance: 16 miles
Highlights: Marinas, military installations, memorials and markets along Washington's waterfront.

No one would characterize Washington as a port city, but it does have a historic and lively waterfront, and cycling provides a great way to tour it. This tour begins at the Eastern Market Metro stop on Capitol Hill, passes the Marine Barracks and the home of the Corps commandant, and pays a visit to the historic Washington Navy Yard, with its museums and a destroyer that visitors can board. The trip continues to a picturesque marina on the southwest waterfront, to the National War College and homes of the Army brass at Fort Lesley J. McNair, and to the part of the waterfront that was "concretized" during the urban renewal craze of the 1950s. After a stop at the pungent Maine Avenue Fish Market and a ride around Haines Point, the tour takes in the Tidal Basin and the Jefferson Memorial and returns to the starting point via the Mall and the Smithsonian Museums.

0.0 From the Eastern Market Metro stop, proceed to the corner of Pennsylvania Avenue and Eighth Street SE and turn right, heading south on Eighth Street.

> 0.2 On your left, at the corner of G Street SE, is the home of the commandant of the U.S. Marine Corps. The house dates from 1805 and is surrounded by the red brick Marine Barracks and the parade grounds.

0.5 Eighth Street ends. Cross M Street SE at the light. You'll be at the ceremonial gate to the Washington Navy Yard. As this entrance is used only by residents and VIPs, turn left on M Street.

0.7 Turn right and enter the Navy Yard through the public gate. Follow the

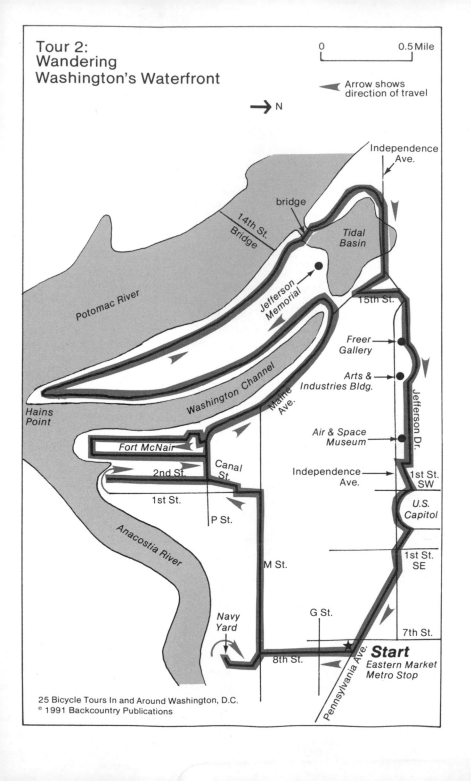

Tour 2:
Wandering
Washington's Waterfront

0   0.5 Mile

Arrow shows
direction of travel

→ N

Independence
Ave.

bridge

14th St.
Bridge

Tidal
Basin

Potomac River

Jefferson
Memorial

15th St.

Freer
Gallery

Arts &
Industries Bldg.

Washington Channel

Maine Ave.

Jefferson Dr.

Hains
Point

Air & Space
Museum

Fort McNair

Canal
St.

2nd St.

Independence
Ave.

1st St.
SW

U.S.
Capitol

1st St.

P St.

Anacostia River

M St.

1st St.
SE

Navy
Yard

G St.

7th St.

8th St.

★ Start
Eastern Market
Metro Stop

Pennsylvania Ave.

25 Bicycle Tours In and Around Washington, D.C.
© 1991 Backcountry Publications

signs to the historic district, and you'll come to the old Commandant's Office.

During the Civil War, this two-story frame building with wraparound porches also served as the home of Commandant John Dahlgren. Lincoln used to come here late at night to play cards. Just behind the Commandant's Office is the Navy Museum, which occupies one of the buildings of the gun factory that once made much of the ammunition and weapons used by the Navy. The museum chronicles the history of the U.S. Navy from the Revolution to the present, and exhibits include gun decks, a submarine room with working periscopes, and historical memorabilia. Admission is free, and the museum is open daily.

Across the parking lot, in a long, low, narrow building where the Navy once tested model ships, is a museum devoted to the history of submarines. In Willard Park, in front of the Navy Museum, is an outdoor display of military weapons and hardware, plus a few picnic tables. At the Anacostia River waterfront is the U.S.S. *Barry,* a destroyer commissioned in 1956 and now a permanent visit ship at the Navy Yard. The *Barry,* which saw action in waters off Cuba and Vietnam, is open daily for self-guided tours. After your tour, backtrack to the gate.

1.6 Turn left on M Street SE. Watch for traffic. After crossing South Capitol Street, you'll be in the southwest quadrant of the District.

2.7 Turn left on First Street SW.

2.8 Turn right on Canal Street and, at P Street, make a left on Second Street. Continue down Second Street past the side of Fort McNair.

3.7 On your right is the James Creek Marina, a perfect place to rest and watch the boats bobbing in the water. There are picnic tables shaded by tall oaks, a soda machine, and ducks to feed. There's a great view of the National War College (across the water).

After your respite, double back on Second Street.

4.4 Turn left on P Street.

Note the bayonet motif on the top of the red brick wall surrounding Fort McNair.

4.6 Turn left and stop at the checkpoint at the main gate of Fort McNair. You must show a picture ID to enter. Bear right around the parade ground then left in front of the gracious brick houses—homes of the Army's top generals—that back on the Washington Channel.

5.1 At the Officer's Club, turn right and then left, following the road that runs along the breakwater.

5.3   The road veers left and leads to the massive Beaux Art building
designed by Stanford White which houses the National War College.

> Before following it, you may want to pause on a bench between the
> water and the golf course and drink in the view of Haines Point and
> of Alexandria in the distance across the Potomac. After passing the
> War College, the road curves to the left and leads you along the
> other side of the parade ground, past the homes of noncommis-
> sioned officers.

6.4   Leave Fort McNair via the main gate and turn left. Follow the sidewalk,
which leads into a pedestrian crossing between apartment buildings.

> 6.5 The Titanic Memorial (left) honors the men who gave up their
> places on the lifeboats and died in the Titanic disaster. The granite
> figure, which represents self-sacrifice, was sculpted by Gertrude
> Vanderbilt Whitney.

6.5   The walkway turns right here, following the waterfront past docks
where the fireboats, marine police boats, and excursion vessels are
moored and on past several large marinas.

> Some of the restaurants that line the waterfront have seasonal out-
> door-seating areas.

7.4   The walkway ends, but continue straight across the parking lot into the
Maine Avenue Fish Market.

> The fish are all trucked in now and sold from boats permanently
> moored here. Exit the fish market and continue in the same direc-
> tion, past a marine store, on the sidewalk which leads under a
> bridge.

7.9   Follow the sidewalk around to the left and enter East Potomac Park,
riding past the tennis bubble, swimming pool, and miniature golf
course on the road alongside the Washington Channel.

> Fort McNair and the southwest waterfront restaurants now lie across
> the channel.

10.0   At the end of the road is Hains Point.

> The Point is marked by cedars and a sculpture known as the
> Awakening, which consists of a half-buried bronze figure. Play-
> grounds, picnic tables, rest rooms, and water are available here.
>
> **Follow the road back along the other side of the peninsula,
> along the Potomac River.**
>
> You'll see a lot of people fishing, and you'll get a good view of planes
> taking off from National Airport across the river.

12.0   After passing under the 14th Street Bridge, carry your bike up the set

Young cyclists enjoy a bird's-eye view of the famed cherry blossoms around Washington's Tidal Basin.

of steps to your right and cross the bridge over the Tidal Basin. Follow either the road or the walkway along the Tidal Basin, which is lined with cherry trees and filled with pedal boats.

To your right is the Jefferson Memorial. Across the road to the left, you're likely to see a rugby or cricket match in progress.

12.6   At the fork, bear right, following the sign for Independence Avenue. At Independence Avenue turn right and cross the bridge over the Tidal Basin. When the road divides, bear right along the basin on Maine Avenue, past the entrance to the pedal boat concession.

13.5   Turn left on 15th Street, crossing at the light. You'll climb a slight hill, past the Bureau of Printing and Engraving where folding money is printed and past the future site of the Holocaust Museum.

13.7   Cross Independence Avenue and turn right on Jefferson Drive, which runs along the Mall.

> 14.0 The Freer Gallery (right) houses Oriental art and paintings by American artists. Of particular interest is the Peacock Dining Room designed for a home in London by James Whistler. Adjacent to the Freer, behind the red brick Smithsonian "castle," is a Victorian garden and the entrance to underground museums devoted to Far Eastern and African art.
>
> 14.3 The Arts and Industries Building (right) contains artifacts from the nation's centennial exposition held in 1876 in Philadelphia. Next door is the Hirschorn Gallery and (left) its outdoor sculpture garden, the centerpiece of which is Auguste Rodin's *Burghers of Calais.* Jefferson Drive continues past the National Air and Space Museum, which has indoor and outdoor cafes, and the Botanical Gardens.

15.0   At the end of Jefferson Drive, cross First Street SW and enter the Capitol grounds, climbing Capitol Hill. At the top of the hill, bear right and exit the grounds at the corner of First Street SE and Independence Avenue. Turn left on Independence Avenue.

15.6   Independence Avenue veers left. Keep right on Pennsylvania Avenue SE.

> On your right are the Chesapeake Bagel Bakery and Sherrill's Bakery, both good, informal eating places. In the next block are a fast-food-chain restaurant, a Thai-Italian restaurant, a Greek taverna, and other food establishments.

16.0   Eastern Market Metro station is on your right, at the corner of Pennsylvania Avenue and Seventh Street SE.

Bicycle Repair Service
Metropolis Bike and Scooter, 719 Eighth Street SE, (202-543-8900)
Southeast Cycle Shop, 629 Pennsylvania Avenue SE, (202-543-5533)

3.

Cycling around Capitol Hill

Location: The northeast and southeast quadrants of the District of Columbia
Terrain: Mainly flat
Road conditions: Paved roads, mainly with light traffic
Distance: 6.6 miles
Highlights: Union Station, the Capitol, the Library of Congress, Christ Church, the Gary Hart house, Eastern Market, Philadelphia Row, Congressional Cemetery, the Folger Library and Theatre.

In Pierre L'Enfant's grand plan for Washington, the city was supposed to grow eastward from the Capitol, which is one reason the Statue of Freedom on top of the Capitol dome faces east. Had things happened as L'Enfant envisioned them, the quiet neighborhood known before the construction of the Capitol as Jenkins Hill would probably have been obliterated. But since commercial and fancy residential development traveled west from the Capitol, Jenkins Hill survives, although it is now called Capitol Hill. This tour, which may be combined with Tour 1 (monuments) or Tour 2 (waterfront), takes you from monumental Washington to small-town Washington. En route, you'll see places where famous, infamous, and ordinary Washingtonians have lived, worshipped, shopped, and died.

The tour begins at Union Station, which has both a Metro station and a parking lot, as well as shops and restaurants.

0.0   Leave Union Station, crossing Massachusetts Avenue in the pedestrian crosswalk in front of the Columbus fountain. Continue up Delaware Avenue.

0.4   Cross Constitution Avenue and enter the Capitol grounds.
There are bike racks on either side of the building if you want to take a tour or just look at the view of the Mall from the West Terrace.

0.5   In front of the dome, turn left to the exit onto First Street NE. Then turn right on First Street.
On your left is the Library of Congress' Jefferson Building. The

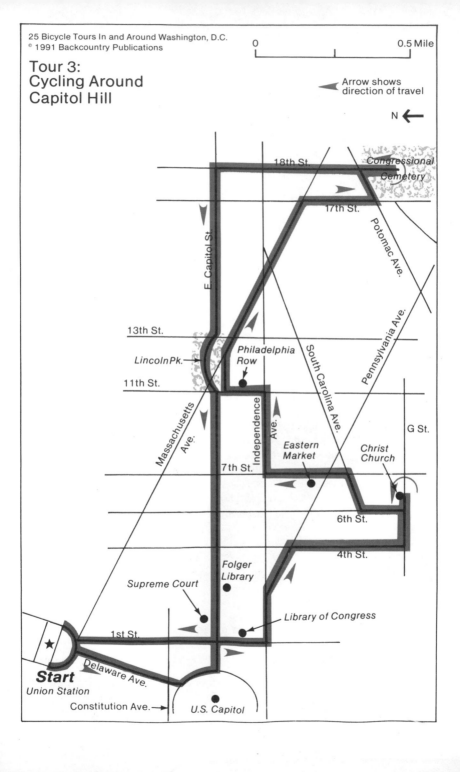

25 Bicycle Tours In and Around Washington, D.C.
© 1991 Backcountry Publications

0   0.5 Mile

Tour 3:
Cycling Around
Capitol Hill

Arrow shows
direction of travel

N ←

18th St.

Congressional
Cemetery

17th St.

E Capitol St.

Potomac Ave.

13th St.

Lincoln Pk.

Philadelphia
Row

Pennsylvania Ave.

11th St.

Massachusetts Ave.

Independence Ave.

South Carolina Ave.

G St.

Eastern
Market

Christ
Church

7th St.

6th St.

4th St.

Folger
Library

Supreme Court

Library of Congress

1st St.

Delaware Ave.

Start
Union Station

Constitution Ave. →

U.S. Capitol

ornate Renaissance architecture alone makes the Jefferson Building well worth a visit, and it also features Gutenberg Bibles, Stradivarius instruments, and changing exhibitions. The Court of Neptune Fountain, in front of the building, is reminiscent of Rome's Fountain of Trevi.

0.6 Turn left on Independence Avenue, in front of the Library's contemporary Madison Building, which also offers changing exhibits.

Just past the Madison Building, bear right on Pennsylvania Avenue, where you'll find several shops and restaurants. Sherrill's Bakery, at 233 Pennsylvania Avenue SE, was the subject of a documentary film that was nominated for an Oscar.

1.0 Turn right on Fourth Street, which has a marked bike lane.

1.3 Turn left on G Street.

1.5 On your left is Christ Church, which was designed by Capitol architect Benjamin Latrobe in 1805 in the Gothic Revival style. Presidents Jefferson, Madison, and John Quincy Adams worshipped here and, much later, John Philip Sousa conducted the choir.

1.5 Turn around and double back half a block to Sixth Street. Turn right on Sixth Street.

1.6 The house at 517 Sixth Street (left) is the one where the press tracked Gary Hart and Donna Rice.

1.7 Turn right on South Carolina Avenue.

On your left, at 630 South Carolina Avenue, stands "The Maples," built in 1795 and once the home of Francis Scott Key. It is now a settlement house.

1.8 Turn left on Seventh Street and cross Pennsylvania Avenue.

1.9 On your left is the Eastern Market, built in 1871 and the last of three such markets envisioned under the L'Enfant Plan. The market holds vegetable, meat, bakery, and fish stands and a restaurant noted for its crab cakes and blueberry pancakes. On Saturdays, farmers sell produce outside the market, competing for space with vendors of crafts and clothing. On Sundays, an active flea market springs up outside. The north end of the market houses an art gallery. Across Seventh Street are restaurants, food shops, antique shops, and other stores.

2.0 Turn right on Independence Avenue.

2.3 Turn left on 11th Street.

The flat-fronted, Greek Revival–style houses on the right side of the street are known collectively as Philadelphia Row. They were designed in 1856 by George Gessford in the style of his native city.

2.4   Turn right on East Capitol Street, which skirts Lincoln Park.

2.6   At the end of the park, bear right on Massachusetts Avenue SE.

3.1   Turn right on 17th Street SE.

3.4   Turn left on Potomac Avenue to the entrance to Congressional Cemetery.

According to art historian James Goode, the cemetery has "the most historic collection of funeral sculpture in the city." Established in 1807 and partially supported by Congressional appropriations, it predated Arlington as a national cemetery. Every member of Congress who died between 1807 and 1877 was memorialized — though not necessarily buried — here by massive, Egyptian-like sandstone monuments designed by Benjamin Latrobe. The practice was stopped after one lawmaker, in a speech from the floor, said that the prospect of being buried under one of these "added new terror to death." You can get a map at the gatekeeper's house or consult one posted outside. Of particular interest are the graves of Civil War photographer Matthew Brady, John Philip Sousa, J. Edgar Hoover, architect of the Capitol William Thornton, several Indian chiefs who died while visiting Washington, and Elbridge Gerry. Lincoln came here in 1864 to the funeral of 21 young women workers killed in a Civil War arsenal explosion. They are buried under a monument paid for by donations from Washingtonians.

4.4   At the cemetery gate, cross Potomac Avenue and continue straight on 18th Street SE.

4.8   Turn left on East Capitol Street.

5.1 On your right is an old trolley car barn that has been turned into condominiums. Look straight ahead for a view of the Capitol dome with the Washington Monument jutting up behind it.

5.3   East Capitol Street turns right to skirt Lincoln Park.

Cross 13th Street and walk through the park to view the Mary McLeod Bethune Memorial, built to honor that black educator. You'll also see the Emancipation Monument, the city's first statue of Lincoln, built in 1876 with money donated by freed slaves.

5.5   Exit the park at East Capitol and 11th Streets. Cross 11th Street in the pedestrian crosswalk and continue west on East Capitol Street, which is framed by an arch of old elms.

Sandstone memorials honor members of Congress in Congressional Cemetery, Washington's first national burying ground.

After the trees have lost their leaves, there's a good view of the Capitol from here. The stately old homes that line the street were built from the 1840s to the early 1900s. In the 1870s, the city began permitting houses with bays. Before that time, houses had to have flat fronts—even now the city technically owns everything up to your front door—even the stoop—in the older sections of the city. So, it's a good bet that the Federal-style flat-fronted houses with the ornate eyebrows over the windows are pre-1870. The houses with bays and intricate brickwork show the influence of the Queen Anne style and date from the 1870s to the 1890s. The Columbian Exposition, held in Chicago in 1893, ushered in a neoclassical revival, so houses built in the late 1890s and early 1900s usually lack intricate brickwork and ornamental detail. Tapestry bricks and red tile roofing are a clue that a house was built in the 20th century. You'll find examples of all these architectural styles, and others, on East Capitol Street.

6.1 On your left is the Folger Shakespeare Library and Theatre. The Great Hall offers changing exhibits, and admission is free. Bas-relief panels on the facade of the building depict scenes from Shakespeare.

6.2 On your right is the U.S. Supreme Court. Visitors may tour the courtroom when the court is not sitting, and there is a small museum in the basement. When the court is in session, visitors must line up to be admitted for short periods. Turn right in front of the court onto First Street NE.

6.6   **Cross Massachusetts Avenue NE and enter Union Station.**

Bicycle Repair Service
Big Wheel Bikes, 315 Seventh Street SE, (202-543-1600)
Southeast Cycle Shop, 629 Pennsylvania Avenue SE, (202-543-5533)

4.

The National Arboretum

Location: The northeast quadrant of the District of Columbia
Terrain: Rolling hills
Road conditions: Busy city streets outside the arboretum. Inside the arboretum, all roads are paved and traffic is light except during peak spring viewing times. (See below.)
Distance: 5 miles if you start from the arboretum parking lot, 9 miles if you start from Stadium-Armory Metro station
Highlights: A delightful sampling of gardens, trees, and views.

The main purpose of the 444-acre National Arboretum is to facilitate government research on trees, shrubs, and herbaceous plants, but it's also a boon to bicyclists who want to take a short, refreshing country ride without leaving the city. You can stop and look at everything or just breeze on through, smelling the blossoms as you pass. Here's a rough idea of what you'll smell — and see — when:

Late March–mid April: Daffodils, magnolias, camellias, quince, rhododendrons, flowering cherries, crab apples

Late April–May: Azaleas, dogwoods, mountain laurel, peonies, old roses, wildflowers, lilacs

June–August: Day lilies, lilies, waterlilies, crape myrtles, herbs

September–October: Deciduous trees put on a fall color show, even the dwarf trees in the Bonsai Collection.

For a Metro start, use Stadium-Armory station, two miles away. From the station, turn left on East Capitol Street, right on 17th Street NE to the intersection with Bladensburg Road. Bear right onto Bladensburg and continue to R Street NE. Turn right on R Street and proceed to the entrance. There is also a large parking lot if you want to drive to the Arboretum. The mileage count begins in the parking lot. Pick up maps and brochures in the Administration Building next to the parking lot before you start.

0.0 Exit the parking lot and turn right onto Azalea Road.

0.2 Turn left on Mount Hamilton Road.

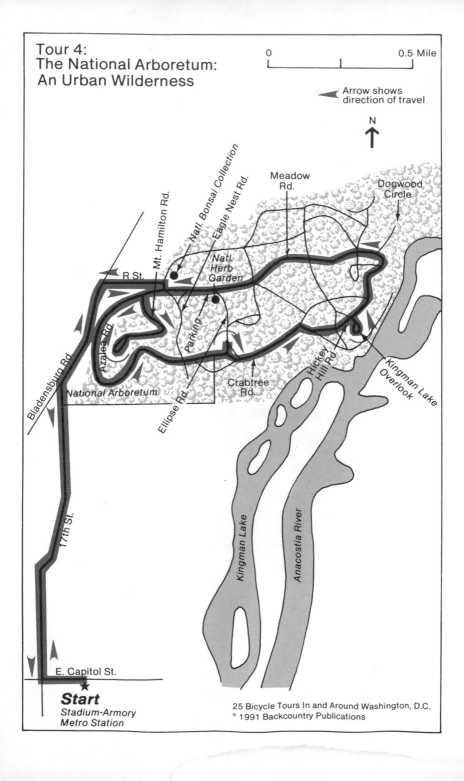

Tour 4:
The National Arboretum:
An Urban Wilderness

0   0.5 Mile

Arrow shows
direction of travel

N

Natl. Bonsai Collection

Eagle Nest Rd.

Meadow
Rd.

Dogwood
Circle

Mt. Hamilton Rd.

Natl.
Herb
Garden

R St.

Azalea Rd.

Parking

Bladensburg Rd.

National Arboretum

Ellipse Rd.

Crabtree
Rd.

Hickey
Hill Rd.

Kingman Lake
Overlook

Kingman Lake

Anacostia River

17th St.

E. Capitol St.

Start
Stadium-Armory
Metro Station

25 Bicycle Tours In and Around Washington, D.C.
© 1991 Backcountry Publications

This road winds up through the azaleas, rhododendrons, and May apples to the top of 239-foot Mount Hamilton. Rest on the bench at the top of the "mountain" and drink in the view of the Capitol, the Library of Congress, the Washington Monument, the Washington Cathedral, and the Shrine of the Immaculate Conception.

0.6   Proceed down the mountain and back to Azalea Road.

1.0   Go left on Azalea road.

On your left you'll see azalea-strewn Mount Hamilton; on your right, crab apple trees. The Morrison Azalea Garden, at the intersection with Eagle Nest Road features a study collection of large-flowered Japanese hybrids. After the intersection, Azalea Road becomes Crabtree Road.

2.1   Turn left on Ellipse Road to a majestic and picturesque "ruin" created from the Corinthian columns removed from the U.S. Capitol during renovation of the east front during the Kennedy administration.

The 14-ton columns were designed by Benjamin Latrobe. Set on this hill and surrounded by understated gardens, they form the closest thing to the Acropolis this side of Athens.
Return to Crabtree Road.

2.9 Fern Valley (left) features a self-guided nature trail along a stream, over a bridge, and past witch hazel, ferns, oaks, wild ginger, bloodroot, trilliums, Dutchman's breeches, stunted American chestnuts, mountain laurel, and hemlocks. Lock your bike in the rack provided.

3.1 Beech Spring Pond is home to ducks and other waterfowl. Its banks are lined with weeping willows.

3.1   Don't take the road that skirts the pond. Instead, bear right on Hickey Hill Road. Then continue on Hickey Hill Road.

3.3   Take the overlook loop (right) to the Kingman Lake Overlook high above the Anacostia River.

3.5 Lock your bike in the rack and take the path through the camellias and the Asian collections to the cinnabar Chinese tea house, which overlooks a man-made waterfall cascading down into the Anacostia River. There's a rest room and a drinking fountain near the bike rack.

3.5   Follow Hickey Hill Road as it curves to the left.

4.0 Park your bike in the rack adjacent to Dogwood Circle and walk the trail that winds through the woods. Then walk across the road to

Corinthian columns removed from the east front of the Capitol grace a hill in the 444-acre National Arboretum.

the Gotelli Dwarf and Slow-growing Conifer Collection, about 1,500 tiny trees in a landscaped setting.

4.0 Back on your bike, follow Meadow Road down the hill, past the crape myrtles (left), past Heart Pond, named for its shape (right), over the bridge that spans Hickey Run.

4.7 Just past the intersection with Ellipse Road, stop to tour the National Bonsai Collection on your right, a Bicentennial gift from Japan.
Some of the tiny trees are hundreds of years old. There are both evergreen and deciduous trees in the collection. The latter lose their leaves in the fall, just as big trees do. The National Herb Garden, on your left, is a fascinating collection of herbs used for medicinal and culinary purposes. In the same area is a collection of old roses.

5.0 Return to the parking lot.

Bicycle Repair Service
Southeast Cycle, 629 Pennsylvania Avenue SE, (202-543-5533)

5.

Pedaling through Rock Creek Park

Location: Northwest Washington and Montgomery County, Maryland
Terrain: Almost flat
Road conditions: A paved, off-road bike trail and a few light-traffic streets
Distance: 16 miles
Highlights: Rock Creek Park, the National Zoo, Pierce Mill, the Miller Cabin, Meadowbrook Stables, the Mormon Temple.

More than a hundred years ago, Washington leaders had the foresight to set aside a wide swath of the city along the banks of Rock Creek as public parkland. Moreover, they had the good sense to leave most of it in its natural state. And, from the beginning, Washingtonians took advantage of their park, with picnics on hot days on the rocks that jut up out of the creek, with hikes to view the wild dogwood that still grows in the park, and even with biking expeditions. One of the park's prime users was President Theodore Roosevelt, who sometimes led less-than-enthusiastic foreign diplomats on vigorous hikes through the park.

Today, the century-old park welcomes hikers, picnickers, horseback riders—and cyclists. A signed trail runs through the park and continues into parkland in Maryland. Much of the trail is on a paved, separate path that leads away from the road and through wooded areas. Part of the trail uses Beach Drive and other roadways that are closed to automobile traffic on weekends. This tour begins at the Foggy Bottom Metro stop and ends at the Medical Center Metro station in Maryland.

0.0 Leave the Foggy Bottom Metro station via the elevator and turn right across the pedestrian mall. Cross 24th Street.

0.1 Turn left on New Hampshire Avenue NW.

0.2 Turn right on Virginia Avenue NW.
On your left is the Watergate complex, site of the infamous burglary that felled a President.

0.4 Cross Rock Creek Parkway in the pedestrian crossing and turn right on the bike path.

0.7 Across the parkway, on your right, stand the ruins of the Godey Lime Kilns, which processed lime brought to Georgetown on the Chesapeake and Ohio Canal from western quarries. The beginning of the canal towpath is on your left. (See tour 6.)

1.0 **The bike path passes under the Buffalo Bridge.**

From underneath you don't see the statue of the bison that gives the bridge its name, but you can see the sandstone faces of an Indian on the arch. The sculptures were reportedly modeled from a death mask of Sitting Bull. The bike path is quite narrow here, and close to the parkway. Use caution.

1.1 On your left is the site of Lyon's Mill, one of 26 mills that used the downrushing waters of Rock Creek. It operated until 1875, and the building was later used as a dance hall.

1.2 The slope on your left is part of Oak Hill Cemetery, final resting place of many of Washington's elite. The white-columned memorial that looks like the Temple of Vesta is the mausoleum of Marcia Burns Van Ness, who died in the devastating cholera epidemic of 1832. There is no access to the cemetery from the bike trail.

1.5 **On your left is an exercise course for those who want to stop to do**

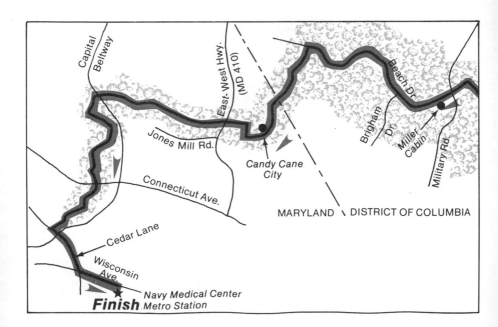

chin-ups and other exercises. Follow the trail signs carefully from this point, crossing the parkway in the pedestrian crossing.

2.5 The path comes to a tunnel. You may go through the tunnel on your bike, but it's much more pleasant to take the alternate route to the left, which leads to the National Zoo.

2.8 Lock your bike in the rack here if you want to visit the zoo.
No bikes are allowed in the zoo, which was created by an act of Congress in 1899 in order to house the animals that were given to the nation by visiting heads of state. Today, the zoo is committed to sheltering its residents in humane and natural settings, to saving endangered species, and, where possible, to returning animals to the wild. Admission is free. After your visit, return to the bike trail—not on the path you entered on but the one that goes off to the left. This will allow you to avoid the tunnel.

3.1 Turn left on the bike trail.

3.8 The bike trail crosses a low, rail-less bridge over the creek. Walk your bike.

3.9 The trail passes under a low bridge then through a wooded area filled with May apples in spring. The path then comes close to the parkway.

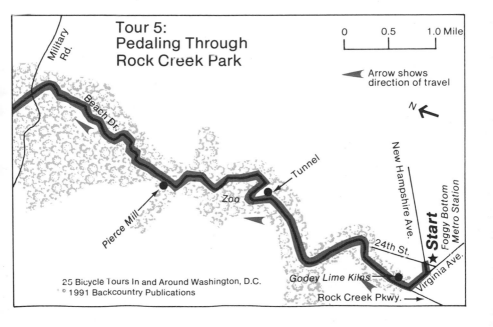

Tour 5:
Pedaling Through
Rock Creek Park

0   0.5   1.0 Mile

◀ Arrow shows direction of travel

N

Military Rd.

Beach Dr.

Tunnel

Zoo

Pierce Mill

New Hampshire Ave.

Foggy Bottom Metro Station

Start

24th St.

Virginia Ave.

Godey Lime Kilns

Rock Creek Pkwy. ▶

25 Bicycle Tours In and Around Washington, D.C.
© 1991 Backcountry Publications

On this stretch, just before the path veers left to cross a wood-railed bridge, glance to your right across the parkway. A sculpted bench on a slight rise honors Henri Jusserand, a French diplomat, and is placed near the spot where Jusserand, newly accredited to Washington, reluctantly forded the creek while on a forced tramp with President Theodore Roosevelt. Following TR's lead, he wrote in a dispatch to the Quai D'Orsay, "I, too, for the honor of France removed my apparel, everything except my lavender kid gloves. The President cast an inquiring look at this as if they, too, must come off, but I quickly forestalled any remark by saying, 'With your permission, Mr. President, I will keep these on; otherwise it would be embarrassing if we should meet ladies.' "

4.6 Pierce Mill, on your left, is open Wednesday through Sunday, 8 a.m. to 4:30 p.m. The sole survivor of the 26 mills that once thrived along Rock Creek, it has been restored. You can watch corn and wheat being ground and buy some of the corn meal and wheat flour. The Art Barn, adjacent to the mill, is an old carriage house that exhibits works of local artists. Rest rooms and drinking fountains are also available here.

5.0 The off-road trail ends and a signed bikeway on Beach Drive, which is closed to cars on weekends, begins. Follow Beach Drive, past the sites of the Blagden and Argyle Mills.

6.6 After passing a park police station with rest rooms (right), Beach Drive crosses Military Road. Cars are allowed on Beach Drive past this point, but there is now a paved bike path.

7.1 On your left is the log Miller Cabin, built by rough-hewn Joaquin Miller, "the poet of the Sierras." The California State Society moved the cabin here from its original site in Meridian Hill Park on 16th Street. Occasional poetry readings are held here.

7.6 At Brigham Drive, the off-road bike path ends. Follow Beach Drive, a signed bike route.

9.1 Follow Beach Drive as it turns left and enters Maryland.

10.4 At Candy Cane City, a large playground and recreation facility, walk your bike up some steps at the entrance and enter the bike path that goes through the playing fields and turns to the right, then makes a sharp left past Meadowbrook Riding Stable.

10.9 The path crosses East-West Highway (MD 410) and continues, skirting a playground then entering the woods and passing under an old wooden trestle. The trail traverses a marsh then leads you through a piney woods.

The Rock Creek trail leads cyclists to Pierce Mill, sole survivor of 26 grist mills powered by the creek's waters.

12.2 The trail emerges from the woods and parallels Jones Mill Road.
If you look straight ahead, you will see the Oz-like towers of the Mormon Temple.

12.5 After crossing under the Capital Beltway, the bike path turns left on Beach Drive.

13.9 The path takes you through a tunnel under Connecticut Avenue. You are following Rock Creek here, and there are picnic tables along its banks.

14.7 At the intersection with Cedar Lane, turn left, leaving the Rock Creek trail and passing under the Beltway again.

14.9 Turn right onto a paved bike path that leads you through pretty backyards and away from the busy street.

15.2 The bike path reemerges on Cedar Lane but continues on a paved path to the side.

15.4 At the intersection with Wisconsin Avenue (MD 355), turn left, crossing Cedar Lane and walking your bike on the sidewalk past Stone Ridge Country Day School and the Naval Medical Center.

Note the medical center's tower, a fine example of "streamlined moderne" architecture. It was completed in 1940. A few years later, James Forrestal, Secretary of the Navy in the Truman administration, jumped to his death from one of the tower windows.

16.0 Cross Wisconsin Avenue in the pedestrian crossing and enter the Medical Center Metro station.

Bicycle Repair Service

Chevy Chase Bicycle Service, 5614 Connecticut Avenue NW, Washington, DC, (202-966-2705)

The Bicycle Place, 10219 Old Georgetown Road, Bethesda, Maryland, (301-530-0100)

6.

Cycling along the C & O Canal

Location: The District of Columbia and Montgomery County, Maryland
Terrain: Flat to moderately hilly
Road conditions: Hard-packed dirt trail with one bad section, paved trail, paved roads, some with moderately heavy traffic
Distance: 26.1 miles
Highlights: The Chesapeake and Ohio Canal, Potomac River views, Clara Barton National Historical Site, Glen Echo Park, the Old Anglers Inn, Great Falls Tavern.

The Chesapeake and Ohio Canal, begun in 1828, stretches from the mouth of Rock Creek in Georgetown to Cumberland, Maryland, some 185 miles to the northwest. An elevated towpath, built 12 feet wide to accommodate the mule teams that pulled the canal barges, now accommodates hikers, joggers, horseback riders—and cyclists. It's possible to bike the entire 185 miles, but this tour takes you from Georgetown, past the first 14 locks of the canal, to Great Falls Tavern Visitors' Center, which offers rides in a mule-drawn replica of the early canal boats and tours of the hostelry that once sheltered canal travelers. From Great Falls you can either double back on the towpath or follow the route to the Rockville Metro station. Since it was rail transportation that made canals obsolete and, indirectly at least, allowed them to become recreational resources, this second choice seems particularly fitting.

The mileage count for this tour begins at the Foggy Bottom Metro station. For an automobile start, there is limited parking at Thompson's Boat Center on Rock Creek Parkway at Virginia Avenue NW. The boat center also rents bikes.

0.0 Exit the Foggy Bottom Metro station via elevator and proceed across the plaza. Cross 24th Street and turn left on New Hampshire Avenue NW.

The small brick rowhouses on this street show what the whole Foggy Bottom neighborhood looked like before it was replaced by high-rise apartment houses and George Washington University buildings.

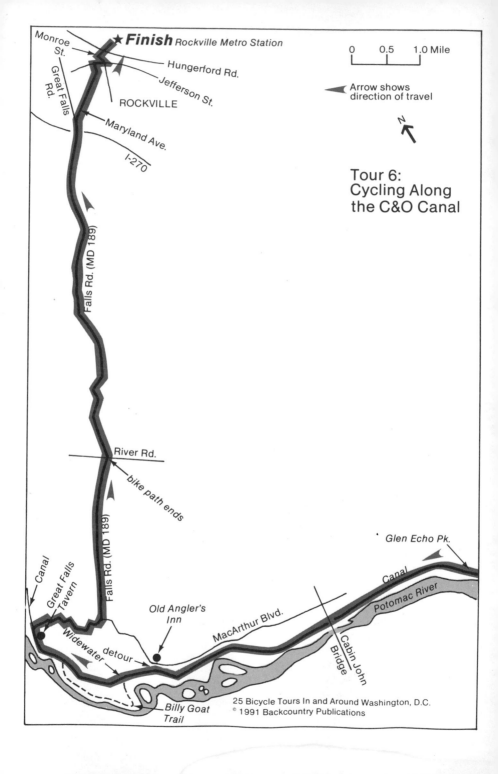

★ **Finish** Rockville Metro Station

Monroe St.

Hungerford Rd.

Great Falls Rd.

Jefferson St.

ROCKVILLE

Maryland Ave.

I-270

0   0.5   1.0 Mile

Arrow shows direction of travel

N

Tour 6:
Cycling Along
the C&O Canal

Falls Rd. (MD 189)

River Rd.

bike path ends

Falls Rd. (MD 189)

Glen Echo Pk.

Canal

Canal

Great Falls Tavern

Potomac River

Old Angler's Inn

MacArthur Blvd.

Widewater

detour

Cabin John Bridge

Billy Goat Trail

25 Bicycle Tours In and Around Washington, D.C.
© 1991 Backcountry Publications

0.2   Turn right on Virginia Avenue.

The posh, notorious Watergate complex is on your left.

0.4   Cross Rock Creek Parkway in the pedestrian crossing and turn right in front of Thompson's Boat Center, onto the Rock Creek bike trail.

0.7   A historical marker on your left indicates the beginning of the C & O Canal towpath. Turn left and follow the paved towpath through Georgetown.

You'll pass four lift locks, the embarkation point for the mule-powered boat that takes visitors on short canal rides, and some old brick houses now painted in rainbow colors and used as artists' studios and shops. One offers carry-out food and ice-cream cones.

1.6   At 34th Street the towpath crosses the canal on a bridge and becomes a dirt trail.

Here the canal is lined with old warehouses and industrial buildings that have been turned into smart shops and condominiums.

1.7 After passing under Key Bridge, you'll see the Victorian-style clubhouse of the Washington Canoe Club on your left. Busy Canal Road is on your right across the canal. Just beyond this point, Canal Road ceases to be a major thoroughfare, and the towpath becomes quieter, more country-like.

3.8 On your left, Fletcher's Boat House offers bike, canoe, and boat rentals and a snack bar. There are picnic tables and a pleasant lawn that leads down to a cove on the Potomac River.

4.5   Cross a wooden bridge over a canal spillway.

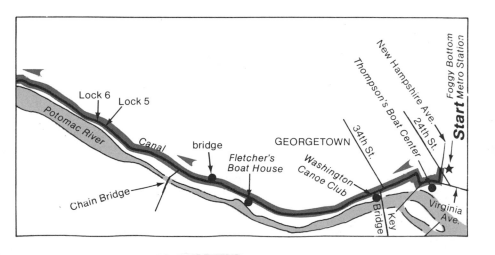

5.7   At Lock #5, the towpath crosses a bridge. Rest rooms and a drinking
fountain are available here.

6.1 The small, whitewashed house provided for the tender of Lock
#6 is typical of these four-room residences, which were part of the
compensation for the tenders. A one-acre garden plot came with the
house. In addition, the canal company paid a salary that ranged
from $100 a year to $75 a month. Boats signalled the tender with a
bugle. In the canal's heyday in the 1870s, an average of more than a
hundred boats a day passed through the locks. In 1835 the canal
company's board ruled against hiring women to tend locks, feeling
that the work was too strenuous. An exception was made for Elizabeth Burgess, who was hired to tend Lock #2 "providing that she
hire a capable assistant."

In this area, the towpath stays close to the Potomac River,
affording views of Little Falls Dam just upstream. Heed the posted
warnings about staying out of the dangerous river.

7.1 On your left is the private Sycamore Island Club.

7.8   A wooden footbridge on your right leads across the canal to Glen Echo
Park and the Clara Barton House.

Lock your bike to the bridge, and, after stopping on the bridge to
watch turtles sunning themselves on the rocks below, follow the
hiking trail that leads to these two attractions. Glen Echo Park, once
a popular amusement park and dance hall, still has a working
antique carousel. The Clara Barton House, made from lumber sal-
vaged from the Johnstown flood, contains memorabilia of the
founder of the American Red Cross.

10.1   Just after passing Lock #13, the towpath goes under the Cabin John
Bridge.

On your right after the bridge is the David Taylor Model Basin, used
by the Navy to test the seaworthiness of ship designs. On your left is
a large picnic area.

13.1   A wide causeway to your right leads to the Old Anglers Inn on Mac-
Arthur Boulevard.

During one of his celebrated hikes to save the canal from being
paved over to create a highway, Justice William O. Douglas
stopped here, with fellow canal aficionados, for lunch. Since the
hikers were not dressed in proper restaurant attire, the management
turned them away. Now, however, the restaurant accommodates
hikers and cyclists with tables placed outside.

The next part of the towpath is not ideal for biking. You may be
forced to carry your bike over boulders and even across flooded

Whitewashed cottages along the Chesapeake and Ohio Canal once housed locktenders and their families.

arcas. However, it's one of the most beautiful sections. As an alternative, leave the towpath here and turn left on MacArthur Boulevard, following the signed bike path to Great Falls Tavern, which is at the end of MacArthur Boulevard.

13.3 A beautiful expanse of wide, lake-like water is on your right. This is a favorite spot for bird watchers. On your left is the entrance to the Billy Goat Trail, a popular hiking route along Mather Gorge. Here, the towpath leads through an area of huge grey boulders and a stark, New England-like landscape. Unfortunately, beauty comes at a price. The towpath is strewn with rocks and washed away in places. For current conditions, call 301-299-3613.

15.0 Great Falls Tavern Visitors' Center offers mule-boat rides, hiking trails, a bookstore, a water fountain, rest rooms, and a museum. Constructed as housing for the tenders of Locks #19 and #20 just upstream, the tavern later became a hotel. The rooms are furnished in 19th-century style. There is an overlook on the river here, but the best views of Great Falls are from the Virginia side. (See Tour 10.)

15.1 Just past the tavern, take the exit road to the right. This is MacArthur Boulevard. Watch for traffic on this winding road.

16.4 Turn left on Falls Road (MD 189), entering the bike path on the right side of the road.

  The path, largely shielded from the road by trees and other vegetation, leads through the tracts of million-dollar homes that make up Potomac, Maryland.

18.4 The bike path ends just before the intersection with River Road (MD 190). Cross River Road and Falls Road in the pedestrian crossings. Food is available in several shops at this intersection. Continue north on Falls Road, watching for traffic.

  19.4 On your left is the Normandie Farms Restaurant, an important meeting place in the quintessential Washington power novel, *Advise and Consent.*

24.0 Falls Road gains a sidewalk here. Take it across the overpass over I-270. When it descends, Falls Road becomes Great Falls Road.

24.7 At the intersection of Great Falls Road and Maryland Avenue, bear right on Maryland Avenue.

25.4 At the county courthouse, turn right on East Jefferson Street.

25.6 Turn left on Monroe Street. Follow it as it turns to the right.

26.1 Cross Hungerford Drive at the light and enter the Rockville Metro station.

Bicycle Repair Service
The Bicycle Pro Shop, 3413 M Street NW, Washington, DC, (202-337-0311)
The Bicycle Place, 855B Rockville Pike, Rockville, Maryland, (301-340-6440)

Virginia Tours

7.

Exploring Arlington Cemetery

Location: Arlington County, Virginia
Terrain: Hilly in Arlington Cemetery and Fort Myer, otherwise flat
Road conditions: Paved bike trails and low-traffic roads in Arlington Cemetery
and Fort Myer
Distance: 5.3 miles
Highlights: Theodore Roosevelt Island, Arlington Cemetery, Fort Myer, the
Marine Corps War Memorial, the Netherlands Carillon.

This tour allows cyclists to take advantage of several types of federally
owned land adjacent to the Potomac River, including an island conser-
vatory, parkland along the river, a national cemetery, and a military
installation. Although the distance pedaled is short, you may want to set
aside enough time to take in the sights and wander on foot. It's particularly suitable for families because there are places to stop, things to see,
and little danger from traffic.

The tour begins in the parking lot for Theodore Roosevelt Island,
accessible from the northbound lanes of the George Washington Parkway. There is a Metro connection at the Arlington Cemetery stop.

Either before or after you start your ride, you should cross the
footbridge (no bikes allowed) to the 88-acre island and walk some of the
nature trails that link its various habitats—swamp, marsh, and upland
forest—that are home to 411 types of plants, 76 species of birds, 20
kinds of mammals, and 9 varieties of reptiles. In the center of the island
stands a 17-foot bronze statue of the conservationist president surrounded by fountains, pools, plantings, bridges, and benches. The
island, which is part of the District of Columbia, was called by various
names, including "Analostan," "My Lord's Island," "Barbadoes," and "Mason's Island" before its dedication to Roosevelt in 1932.

0.0 Exit the parking lot and head south along the Mount Vernon bike trail,
which will lead you onto a boardwalk that runs under the Theodore
Roosevelt Bridge and over a duck-filled marsh.

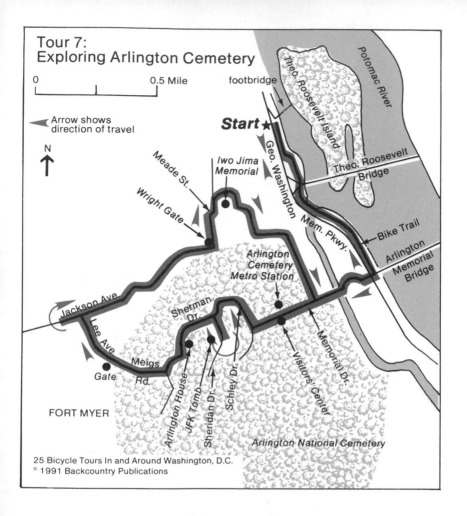

Tour 7:
Exploring Arlington Cemetery

0   0.5 Mile   footbridge

◄ Arrow shows
direction of travel

N
↑

Start ★

Meade St.

Iwo Jima
Memorial

Wright Gate

Geo. Washington Mem. Pkwy.

Theo. Roosevelt Island

Potomac River

Theo. Roosevelt
Bridge

Bike Trail

Arlington
Memorial
Bridge

Arlington
Cemetery
Metro Station

Jackson Ave.

Lee Ave.

Sherman Dr.

Meigs
Gate Rd.

FORT MYER

Arlington House

JFK Tomb

Sheridan Dr.

Schley Dr.

Visitors' Center

Memorial Dr.

Arlington National Cemetery

25 Bicycle Tours In and Around Washington, D.C.
© 1991 Backcountry Publications

0.7   Just after you pass under Arlington Memorial Bridge, there is a green signpost. Follow the directions to Arlington Cemetery, turning right and crossing the highway in the pedestrian crossings. Enter Memorial Drive and continue to the signs for the visitors' center.

        On the left just before the entrance to the visitors' center, stands "The Hiker," a bronze statue of a rough rider memorializing the soldiers of the Spanish-American War.

1.1   Turn left into the entrance to the visitors' center, where maps, rest rooms, and water fountains are available.

        If you want an in-depth tour of the cemetery, you can arrange for one here. Or you can lock up your bike and take a self-guided tour. Since bicycles are only allowed on some cemetery roads, this tour will give you just a sample of the cemetery. The Metro elevator is just across Memorial Drive from the entrance to the visitors' center. If you want to do this trip by Metro, start from the visitors' center. When you exit the visitors' center, turn left and continue to the end of Memorial Drive.

1.2 **Turn right on Schley Drive, which winds uphill, makes a left turn and becomes Sherman Drive.**

No cars are permitted in the cemetery except those of bona fide relatives of people buried here, so traffic is very light.

1.3 On the left is a walk leading to the grave of William Howard Taft and his wife, Helen. An appropriately Edwardian memorial in ornate rose marble, it has shaded benches. Nearby are the starker graves of a whole generation of well-known military leaders: Omar Bradley, Lawton Collins, Earle Wheeler, and others.

1.4 **At the intersection with Sheridan Drive, there's a bike rack and a water fountain. Lock your bike here and walk down Sheridan Drive to the John F. Kennedy and Robert F. Kennedy grave sites. Then continue climbing the hill on Sherman Drive.**

1.6 **Turn left into the entrance for Arlington House.**

Before entering the house, which is open daily for free tours, stop on the portico to enjoy what the visiting Marquis de Lafayette described as the "finest view in the world." Built between 1802 and 1817 by George Washington Parke Custis, a descendant of Martha Washington, the house was named for the ancestral Custis estate on the eastern shore of Virginia. It passed to his daughter, Mary Anna Randolph Custis who married a young West Point graduate named Robert E. Lee. It was here at Arlington House, in his bedroom on the second floor, on the night of April 19, 1861, that Lee made his painful and fateful decision to resign from the U.S. Army and join the Confederate forces. Two days later he left for Richmond, never to return to Arlington House. The estate was confiscated in 1864, and a military cemetery was started on the grounds. After the war, a descendant of the Lees sued the government for return of the property—and won. But, since the military graves surrounding the house made it unattractive as a dwelling place, he accepted a settlement of $150,000.

Of special interest in the mansion is the White Parlor. The decor of this room shows the influence of the time Lee spent in Mexico during the Mexican-American War.

Exit the mansion driveway and turn left, continuing along Sherman Drive.

1.7 **Turn right on Meigs Avenue.**

This road was named for Major General Montgomery Meigs, quar-

The Washington Monument provides a dramatic backdrop for the Mount Vernon bike trail, which connects Arlington Cemetery and Theodore Roosevelt Island.

termaster general of the Union Army, whose idea it was to commandeer the Lee estate for a military cemetery. Meig's vindictive attitude is made more understandable by the fact that his only son, Major John Rodgers Meigs, was killed at the age of 22 in a Virginia skirmish in 1864.

2.0 Pass through the gate to Fort Myer. Meigs Avenue becomes Lee Avenue at the gate. Follow it around to the right.

Just inside the gate, on the Fort Myer side, is a small chapel used for many of the funerals that culminate in burial in Arlington.

2.3   Turn left on Jackson Avenue, in front of the Officers' Club. Continue past the post office.

2.4 On the right are the stables that house the horses used for military funerals and other ceremonies. They are open for free, informal tours daily from 12 to 4 p.m.

2.4   Reverse direction and double back on Jackson Avenue, past the fine old red brick homes of senior army officers and head downhill toward Wright Gate.

3.2   Just beyond the gate, turn left on Meade Street, which leads to the Marine Corps War Memorial, known colloquially as the Iwo Jima monument.

The statue sets in bronze a photograph taken by Associated Press combat photographer Joe Rosenthal, a native Washingtonian. The Pulitzer Prize-winning picture showed six Marines raising the American flag atop Mount Suribachi, the highest point on the small island of Iwo Jima and the scene of bloody fighting in 1945. Three of those Marines survived the battle and later posed for sculptor Felix de Weldon. De Weldon sculpted likenesses of the dead Marines from photographs.

Adjacent to the memorial is the Netherlands Carillon, a gift from the people of the Netherlands in recognition of our aid during World War II.

3.4   Turn right out of the parking lot for the Marine memorial and follow the path that leads in front of the carillon. The path then turns left then right and runs between the red sandstone wall of the cemetery and the Jefferson Davis Highway.

4.0   At the intersection with Memorial Drive, turn left. If you are using Metro, the elevator is to your left. If you are returning to Theodore Roosevelt Island, continue left on Memorial Drive and, using the pedestrian crossings, return to the Mount Vernon bike trail.

4.6   Turn left on the trail.

5.3   Enter the parking lot for Theodore Roosevelt Island.

Bicycle Repair Service
Metropolis Bike and Scooter, The Village at Shirlington, Arlington, Virginia (703-671-1700)

8.

Along the Potomac to Mount Vernon

Location: Northern Virginia
Terrain: Mostly flat with a few gentle hills
Road conditions: A paved, off-the-road bike path except for a short stretch on city streets through the city of Alexandria where there will be light to moderate traffic on weekends
Distance: 28.8 miles
Highlights: Potomac River views, Old Town Alexandria, Dyke Marsh, River Farm, Mount Vernon.

If George Washington had owned a bicycle, this trail to Mount Vernon might have been completed a lot sooner than it was, in 1973. If you ignore the cars zipping by on the George Washington Memorial Parkway

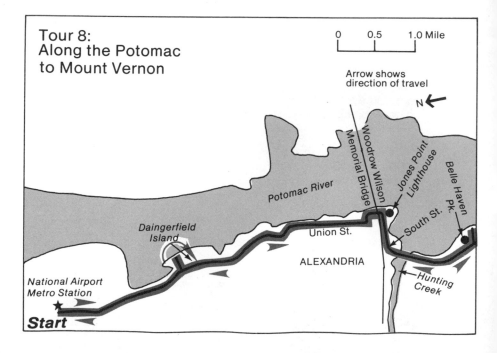

and focus your attention on the river side of the trail, you'll find that the views aren't radically different from those the first president would have seen. The 17-mile trail actually starts at Memorial Bridge, where it connects with the Washington and Old Dominion Railroad Regional Park Trail. (See Tours 10 and 25.) This tour begins a few miles down river at the National Airport Metro stop.

0.0 **Exit the National Airport Metro station and follow signs to the bike trail.**
Although the trip begins in an airport-industrial milieu, the trail soon breaks out into a plethora of pleasant river views. Approaching Daingerfield Island, you seem to sail into the proverbial "forest of masts."

1.3 **Turn left to the Washington Sailing Marina on Daingerfield Island, which is no longer a real island.**
This 107-acre park holds an excellent but rather expensive restaurant, Potomawk Landing, plus picnic tables, rest rooms, water fountains, phones, and playing fields. There is also a large parking lot, which makes this a good starting point for people who prefer car starting points to Metro starting points.

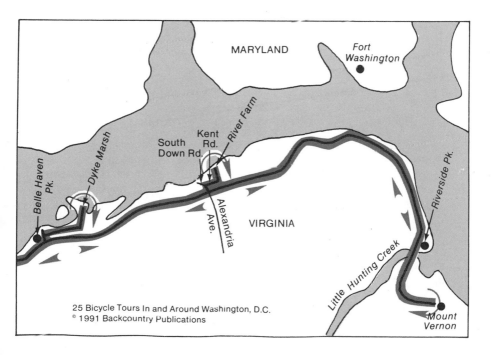

25 Bicycle Tours In and Around Washington, D.C.
© 1991 Backcountry Publications

2.1 The trail breaks temporarily in Old Town Alexandria, but signs guide you along city streets. After passing Ornoco Bay Park, a waterfront area with picnic tables, turn left on Pendleton Street and take an immediate right on North Union Street.

> 3.0 On your left stands the Torpedo Factory, a World War II munitions operation that now houses craft shops, studios, and galleries. Hitch your bike to a street sign and browse, stroll along the waterfront, and walk up King Street (right) for window shopping and information and walking-tour maps at Ramsay House Visitors' Center, 221 King Street. Housed in the home of William Ramsay, a Scottish merchant and city founder, the visitors' center can provide information on and directions to other Old Town attractions, including two homes of Robert E. Lee; Christ Church, attended by both Washington and Lee; Gadsby's Tavern, where Washington used to sip Madeira; and the Stabler Leadbeater Apothecary Museum, where Martha Washington used to buy medicines.

4.0 At Gibbon and Union streets, the off-the-road bike trail resumes, leading you through the woods, back along the river, and past an old Ford plant.

4.3 Keeping left, along the river and under the Wilson Bridge, you'll see the Jones Point Lighthouse, which warned sailors of nearby sandbars from 1836 to 1925. Look along the seawall for the cornerstone that once marked the southernmost corner of the District of Columbia. Turn right and follow the road directly under the Wilson Bridge to South Street. Turn left.

4.8 Turn left on South Washington Street, following the marked trail.
> You'll pass some large apartment complexes, cross Hunting Creek, and be treated to a sweeping vista of the wide Potomac.

5.5 The trail leads through Belle Haven park, site of an 18th-century settlement of Scottish tobacco merchants. Wide green lawns, a marina, picnic tables, and rest rooms are available. Turn left on the road that leads to Belle Haven Marina, and then make an immediate right on a dirt trail that leads through Dyke Marsh.

> Dyke Marsh is a wetland sanctuary and the last large tidal freshwater marsh in the Washington area. Except after very heavy rains, the trail is passable for touring bikes. The first encroachment on the marsh's natural state came in the early 1800s, when a settler tried to turn the wetland into farmland by building earthen dikes around it. These were soon abandoned as too costly, and the land reverted to its natural — wet — state. Ride quietly and you may catch glimpses of frogs, turtles, beavers, muskrats, rabbits, shrews, field mice, foxes, and more than 200 species of birds.

6.2 The Dyke Marsh trail ends at the river. Reverse direction and return to the main bike trail.

6.9 Turn left on the marina road and left again on the Mount Vernon Trail.

7.3 The trail enters a boardwalk that skirts Dyke Marsh.

9.1 The trail exits the woods and enters a small residential enclave. Trail signs direct cyclists across a bridge on Alexandria Avenue, but a short detour will allow a visit to River Farm. Instead of crossing the bridge, continue straight on Southdown Road.

9.2 Bear right on Kent Road.

9.7 Turn left into River Farm, the headquarters of the American Horticultural Society.

> The house dates from 1757 but was much altered in the 1920s. George Washington bought the property in 1760, gave it its name, and later presented it to his personal secretary, Tobias Lear, as a wedding gift. The house is open for special exhibits. The grounds and beautiful gardens are open summer weekends, and the public is welcome to picnic by the river, under trees that Washington may have planted.

A boardwalk carries cyclists and hikers across Dyke Marsh on the Mount Vernon Trail.

9.9   After your visit, reverse direction and return to the intersection of Southdown Road and Alexandria Avenue.

10.7   Turn left and cross the Alexandria Avenue bridge. Once across, turn left again, following the trail signs. The trail stays close to the parkway, skirting some quiet residential neighborhoods, and then enters a wooded area and climbs a hill.

> 12.9 Rest on a bench and drink in the view of Fort Washington, an early 19th-century bastion on the Maryland shore. You'll go up and down a few curvy hills, then cross to the river side of the parkway again.

> 14.7 Riverside Park, at the point where Little Hunting Creek empties into the widest point of the river you've glimpsed so far, offers picnic tables as well as views. Rest up for some uphill climbs and downhill coasts.

15.8   Proceed with caution through the large Mount Vernon parking lot to the mansion entrance, probably with a stop at the rest rooms and snack bar first.

> The mansion is open daily including Christmas, and there is an admission fee. In addition to the mansion itself, which contains the bed where George Washington died, attractions include boxwood gardens, the smokehouse, and the slave burial ground.

> Unless you have arranged for someone to pick you up, you'll have to double back along the trail.

27.5   Arrive at Washington Sailing Marina.

28.8   Arrive at National Airport Metro station.

Bicycle Repair Service
Tow Path Cycle of Alexandria, 823 So. Washington Street, Alexandria, Virginia, (703-549-5368)
Big Wheel Bikes, 2 Prince Street, Alexandria, Virginia, (703-739-2300)
The Bicycle Exchange, 1506-C Belle View Boulevard, Alexandria, Virginia, (703-768-3444)

9.

North Arlington Adventure

Location: Arlington, Virginia
Terrain: Moderately hilly
Road conditions: Bike trails, park roads, and neighborhood streets with light traffic
Distance: 7.3 miles
Highlights: Donaldson Run trail, Potomac Overlook Regional Park and Nature Center, Gulf Branch Nature Center with scenic hiking trail to the Potomac River, Walker Chapel and cemetery.

Arlington, which is actually a county rather than a town or city, is sometimes brushed off as a mere bedroom community for Washington. But it has a character all its own, which has been enlivened in recent years by an influx of refugees from Southeast Asia. An impressive network of bike paths, trails, and parks give what is really an urban area a country-like ambiance — as do the "runs" or streams that riddle the area, flowing down Arlington's hills and into the Potomac River.

This tour takes the rider through some of Arlington's pleasant older neighborhoods, explores the trail that follows the course of Donaldson Run, visits two wooded parks, and includes an optional walk along Gulf Branch to the Potomac. It also allows visits to two nature centers, including one housed in a former love nest of Pola Negri and Rudolf Valentino.

The trip starts at Arlington's Yorktown High School. To get there from the District, cross Key Bridge and turn right on Lee Highway, continuing to the intersection with North George Mason Drive. Turn right onto George Mason Drive; then make an immediate left onto Florida Street. Florida Street ends at 28th Street, in front of the school parking lot.

0.0 Exit the parking lot and turn left on 28th Street.

0.2 Turn right on Yorktown Boulevard.

0.6 After going under an overpass, bear left on 26th Street. Marymount College will be on your left. Immediately after you pass the pungent community leaf-mulch pile on your right, turn right into the woods on the Donaldson Run Trail.

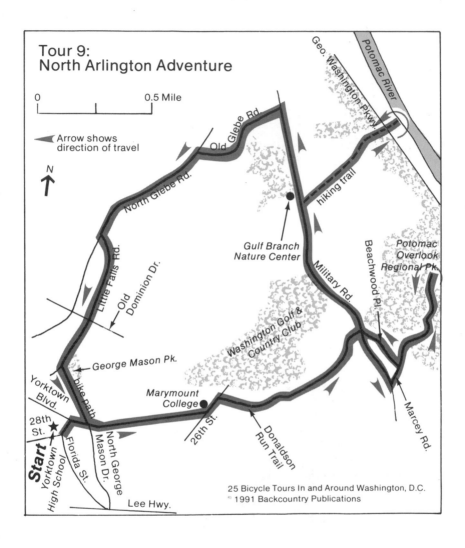

Tour 9:
North Arlington Adventure

0   0.5 Mile

◄ Arrow shows
direction of travel

N

Geo. Washington Pkwy.

Potomac River

Old Glebe Rd.

North Glebe Rd.

hiking trail

Gulf Branch
Nature Center

Little Falls Rd.

Old Dominion Dr.

Military Rd.

Beachwood Pl.

Potomac
Overlook
Regional Pk.

George Mason Pk.

Washington Golf &
Country Club

Yorktown Blvd.

bike path

Marymount
College

26th St.

Donaldson
Run Trail

Marcey Rd.

28th St.

Start

Yorktown High School

Florida St.

North George Mason Dr.

Lee Hwy.

25 Bicycle Tours In and Around Washington, D.C.
© 1991 Backcountry Publications

This mainly downhill trail, which follows the sometimes heavy, sometimes dry stream, emerges briefly into the surrounding neighborhood to cross North Vermont Street, then reenters the woods.

1.6 The trail ends at Military Road. Turn right and make a brief uphill
climb.

1.8 Turn left on Marcey Road, which will lead you into Potomac Overlook
Regional Park.

A cyclist approaches Gulf Branch Nature Center, once a love nest for silent film stars Pola Negri and Rudolf Valentino.

This is a large park that seems miles away from urban and suburban bustle. It has picnic tables, tennis courts, water fountains, rest rooms, a nature center, and a network of hiking trails.

After riding to the end of the paved road, reverse direction and exit the park.

3.2 Turn right on Beachwood Place and follow it to the bottom of a hill, where it runs into Military Road. Bear right on Military Road and bike an up-and-down-hill course past the Washington Golf and Country Club (left).

4.3 Turn left into Gulf Branch Nature Center.

The stone bungalow that houses the nature center once served as a love nest for Pola Negri and Rudolf Valentino. Lock your bike here and take the hiking trail that follows Gulf Branch down to the Potomac. This beautiful walk will take you under the George Washington Parkway for an unobstructed view of the river.

After leaving the nature center, turn left and continued up Military Road.

4.8   Turn left on Old Glebe Road.

4.9 On the left is a marker commemorating the site of Fort Ethan Allen, one of a circle of forts hastily constructed to defend the capital during the Civil War. This one was supposed to command the approaches to nearby Chain Bridge.

5.1 On the right is the cemetery attached to Walker Chapel. The earliest grave marks the resting place of David Walker, who died in 1848. The Walker family donated the land for the cemetery and church, which is Methodist. The current structure replaces a frame country church that was built in 1876.

5.1   Old Glebe Road runs into North Glebe Road. Bear left on North Glebe Road, watching for traffic.

6.3   Just after North Glebe Road makes a left turn, turn right on Little Falls Road. This road will cross Old Dominion Drive and take you past the Rock Spring United Church of Christ.

6.8   Just past the church, turn left on the bike path that leads through George Mason Park.

7.1   The bike path ends at the intersection of North George Mason Drive and Yorktown Boulevard. Turn right onto Yorktown Boulevard.

7.2   Turn right on 28th Street.

7.3   Enter Yorktown High School parking lot.

Bicycle Repair Service
The Bicycle Exchange, 3121 Lee Highway, Arlington, (703-522-1110)

10.

A Great Ride to Great Falls

Location: Northern Virginia
Terrain: Hilly
Road conditions: Paved trail and roads with mainly light traffic
Distance: 36 miles
Highlights: The Great Falls of the Potomac, Riverbend Park, Reston, Vienna, the Washington and Old Dominion Trail.

On its way to the sea from the mountains of West Virginia, the Potomac River really picks up speed as it approaches Washington—dropping 80 feet in less than a mile and roaring through Mather Gorge in a rush of churning white water. This point on the river, known as Great Falls, has long attracted visitors, who come to gaze at the raw power of nature, to picnic, fish, hike, rock climb, or even boat in the white water below the falls. At turn of the century, the Washington and Old Dominion Railroad built a branch line to carry excursionists to the falls, where an inn, a dance pavilion, and a carousel added to the natural attractions. Today the railroad, the inn, the pavilion, and the carousel are gone, but the park is still so popular that the parking lot is sometimes full—and closed to visitors—by noon.

You can avoid Great Falls gridlock by cycling to the falls, on a route that takes advantage of the Washington and Old Dominion Trail—the roadbed of the main line of the railroad to Great Falls—and that travels for a short distance on Old Dominion Drive—the roadbed of the spur to Great Falls. After a visit to Riverbend Park, a quieter spot on the Potomac upstream from the falls, the tour continues through the hills of northern Virginia, runs through the pioneer planned community of Reston, and rejoins the W & OD Trail for a visit to Vienna, a town that has honored its railroad past by restoring a caboose, which stands adjacent to the trail.

Appropriately enough, this tour begins at a Metrorail stop, the Dunn Loring station, which affords easy access to the W & OD Trail.

0.0 Exit the Dunn Loring station, turning left on **Gallows Road.** There is a paved trail along the road.

0.7 Turn left onto the W & OD Trail.

Although it traverses a suburban area, the trail is pleasantly wooded. Watch for wild Turk Cap lilies, which burst into blossom in July.

2.0 A historical marker indicates the spot where the railroad was used during the Civil War to carry a South Carolina regiment to a battle with Ohio volunteers.

3.1 The trail crosses Maple Avenue, the main thoroughfare of Vienna. (Restaurants and food stores are available on this street.) Cross Maple at the stoplight, and continue on the trail.

4.9 Exit the trail to the right through the small parking lot that lies across the trail from the Clarks Crossing soccer field and park. Proceed along Clarks Crossing Road.

5.7 Clarks Crossing Road stops at Beulah Road. Turn left onto Beulah Road.

5.8 At the stop sign, Beulah Road turns left. Cross Old Court House Road and continue straight on Trap Road (VA 676).

6.4 At the stop sign, follow Trap Road to the left, past the Barns at Wolf Trap, part of the Filene Center for the Performing Arts, which is administered by the National Park Service.

6.2 After crossing over the Dulles Access Road on a bridge, Trap Road passes the main part of Wolf Trap Farm Park, location of a popular outdoor summer theater. The park was once the farm of Mrs. Jouett Shouse, who donated it to the nation.

7.7 Trap Road turns right. Follow Towlston Road, which continues straight ahead as VA 676.

8.2 Towlston Road crosses VA 7 and winds through an area of large homes set back from the road.

8.6 Turn left on Peacock Station Road.

8.9 Peacock Station Road ends. Turn left on Old Dominion Drive, following the route the railroad to Great Falls used to take.

10.6 Old Dominion Drive crosses Georgetown Pike and continues down a hill and through the woods into Great Falls Park.

11.5 Stop at the tollbooth to pay a 50-cent-per-bicycle admission fee and to pick up a trail map before proceeding straight ahead to the visitors' center, which has exhibits on the geology and history of the area, plus rest rooms, a snack bar, and a bookstore.

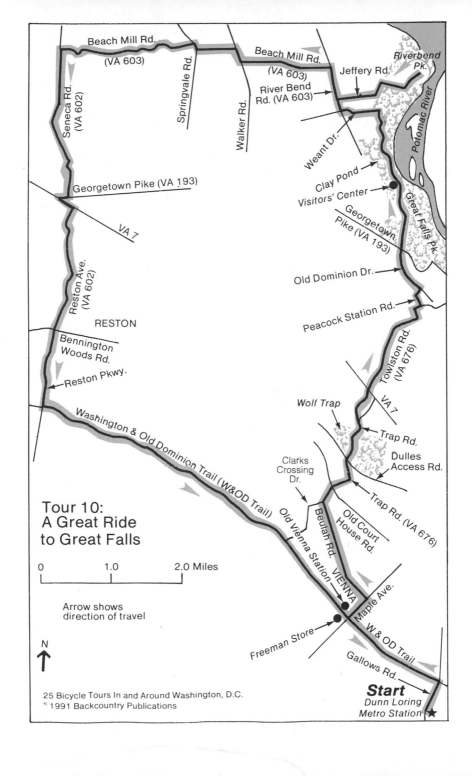

Beach Mill Rd.
(VA 603)

Beach Mill Rd.
(VA 603)

Jeffery Rd.

Riverbend
Pk.

Seneca Rd.
(VA 602)

Springvale Rd.

Walker Rd.

River Bend
Rd. (VA 603)

Weant Dr.

Potomac River

Georgetown Pike (VA 193)

VA 7

Clay Pond

Visitors' Center

Georgetown
Pike (VA 193)

Great Falls Pk.

Reston Ave.
(VA 602)

Old Dominion Dr.

RESTON

Peacock Station Rd.

Bennington
Woods Rd.

Reston Pkwy.

Towlston Rd.
(VA 676)

VA 7

Washington & Old Dominion Trail (W&OD Trail)

Wolf Trap

Trap Rd.

Dulles
Access Rd.

Clarks
Crossing
Dr.

Trap Rd. (VA 676)

Tour 10:
A Great Ride
to Great Falls

0   1.0   2.0 Miles

Old Vienna Station

Beulah Rd.

Old Court
House Rd.

VIENNA

Maple Ave.

Arrow shows
direction of travel

N

Freeman Store

W & OD Trail

Gallows Rd.

25 Bicycle Tours In and Around Washington, D.C.
© 1991 Backcountry Publications

Start
Dunn Loring
Metro Station

Lock your bike at the rack outside the visitors' center and walk to the overlook for a spectacular view of the falls. Look downstream for kayakers daring the white water. Near the observation platforms are ruins of some of the workings on the Patowmack Canal, a pet project of George Washington. Construction on this Great Falls by-pass began in 1786 and was completed two years after Washington died — giving reality to his frequent toast: "Success to the navigation of the Potomac!" Unfortunately, the high cost of building his canal eventually bankrupted the company and the route was abandoned in 1830, leaving the way open for the Chesapeake and Ohio Canal on the Maryland side of the river. (See Tour 6.)

After leaving the visitors' center, continue to the end of the parking lots. On your left, you will see Clay Pond.

11.7   Turn left onto the paved fire road at the head of Clay Pond. It soon turns to easily negotiable dirt and gravel and winds uphill through the woods.

12.7   The trail ends at Weant Drive. Turn left and be prepared for a series of roller-coaster hills.

13.3   Turn right on River Bend Road (VA 603).

13.5   Turn right on Jeffrey Road, which makes a left and then turns right into River Bend Park.

14.3   Proceed past the tollgate (no fee for bikes) to the visitors' center, which has a snack bar and picnic tables on a deck that overlooks a sweeping lawn leading down to the Potomac.

After seeing the fury of Great Falls, you may find it hard to believe that this is the same river only a mile or so upstream. It's quite tranquil here, with boats for rent and a nature center. After a respite in this pretty and peaceful park, double back on Jeffrey Road, riding through the park gates to the intersection with River Bend Road.

16.3   Turn right on River Bend Road.

16.8   River Bend Road ends. Turn left on Beach Mill Road, the continuation of VA 603.

18.3   Beach Mill Road seems to end, but really doesn't. Turn right on Walker Road.

18.4   Turn left and pick up Beach Mill Road again. This is an area of large homes and horse farms.

19.0 At the intersection with Springvale Road stands the Auberge Chez Francois, a very popular French-style country inn, successor to a downtown restaurant. In Sally Quinn's Washington novel, *Regrets Only,* the wife of the vice president begins her illicit relationship with a journalist here, after being smuggled out of the vice-presidential mansion in a garbage can. The restaurant is surrounded by a large garden where some of the herbs used in the kitchen are grown. In off-peak hours, you can sometimes see the help eating outside the kitchen door, a vignette out of a French painting. The restaurant is open for dinner only, but begins serving Sundays at 2 p.m. Jackets and ties are required for men.

19.0 Continue across Springvale Road on Beach Mill Road, which enters a very hilly phase, winding past expensive-looking, brand-new "chateaux," many with For Sale signs.

21.2 Beach Mill Road ends. Turn left on Seneca Road (VA 602).
Look to your right for spectacular views of distant blue mountains.

23.3 Seneca Road ends at Georgetown Pike (VA 193). Follow Georgetown Pike to the right for about a hundred feet and then cross VA 7 at the light. Turn left on VA 7, riding on the shoulder to the frontage road.

23.5 Turn right on Reston Avenue, which is the continuation of VA 602. There is a food store at the intersection. When it enters the thriving "new town" of Reston, Reston Avenue becomes Reston Parkway.
Laid out in 1892 by Dr. Carl Adolph Max Wiehle, who acquired a 7,200-acre tract here with a partner, the town did not become a reality until the early 1960s.

25.3 At the intersection with Bennington Woods Road, a paved bike path begins, parallel to Reston Parkway. It continues, with a few interruptions, to the intersection of Reston Parkway and the W & OD Trail.

26.5 Turn left on the W & OD Trail, which runs through fields and over lowland crisscrossed by small streams.
Listen for frogs and watch for river otters and herons. A stone-arch bridge carries the trail over Piney Branch.

32.7 On your right is the old Vienna railroad station, which is currently leased to the Northern Virginia Model Railroaders Association. These hobbyists are in the process of modeling a section of the Western North Carolina Railroad, complete with operating trains, scenery, and buildings. Several times a year the railroaders hold open house at the old station to show visitors their work in progress. Call 703-938-5157 for dates and information. On the other side of the trail stands a bright red, refurbished caboose, which the town of Vienna acquired after Virginia repealed the law requiring manned cabooses on trains.

32.8 On your left, at the corner of Church Street and the trail, stands the Freeman Store, an emporium that dates to 1859 and is now operated as a general store by Historic Vienna, Inc. It's open Sundays from 12 to 5 p.m. and sells crafts, handmade items and penny

With a mighty roar, the Potomac River careens down the fall line at Great Falls, Virginia.

candy. The house also served as the town's post office and as its first railroad station. During the Civil War, the building was occupied by both Northern and Southern troops as the village, with its strategically important railroad, changed hands frequently.

32.9 **The trail crosses Maple Avenue, Vienna's main artery.**
The town, settled in the 1760s by Scots and originally called Ayr Hill, was rechristened Vienna in 1858 by a doctor who had lived in Vienna, New York, and studied medicine in Vienna, Austria. Although part of the mushrooming Washington suburban area, Vienna retains its small-town charm.

35.3 **Turn right on Gallows Road.**

36.0 **Turn right into the Dunn Loring Metro station.**

Bicycle Repair Service
Nova Cycle, 124 Maple Avenue W, Vienna, Virginia (703-938-7191)

11.

Gunston Gallivant

Location: Fairfax County, Virginia
Terrain: One gradual uphill climb, otherwise flat
Road conditions: A short stretch with moderately heavy traffic along Gunston Road, light traffic on paved park roads
Distance: 9 miles
Highlights: Gunston Hall, Mason Neck State Park

As you make this trip, pretend you are George Mason (1725–1792) making a tour of your 5,000-acre estate. Mason, of course, would have traveled by horse rather than bike, but, except for the cars and power boats, the scene he would have surveyed is much the same: an exquisitely decorated Georgian house, a view of the Potomac River framed by an alleyway of boxwoods, a peninsula populated by bald eagles, hawks, white-tailed deer, foxes, bobcats, and songbirds.

George Mason was a behind-the-scenes statesman, and once you've experienced the serene beauty of his home, Gunston Hall, and surrounding Mason Neck, you'll understand why he eschewed the political hustle and bustle of Philadelphia and Williamsburg for the quiet of his study. Here, in 1776, he penned the Virginia Declaration of Rights, which helped inspire both our Bill of Rights and France's Declaration of the Rights of Man.

The tour begins at Gunston Hall, which is now owned by the state of Virginia. To get there, take I-95 south from Washington to exit 55, which leads to US 1. Take US 1 south to VA 242. Take VA 242 east to Gunston Hall Park at the visitors' center. Either before or after your bike tour, you'll want to tour the house, outbuildings and grounds. There is an admission charge and tours are available daily. Highlights are the Chinese Chippendale dining room and the Palladian parlor, with intricate carved woodwork by an indentured English servant named William Buckland.

0.0 Exit the parking lot and take the entrance road that leads to Gunston Hall back toward Gunston Road.

0.6 Turn left on Gunston Road (VA 600E). Watch for traffic.

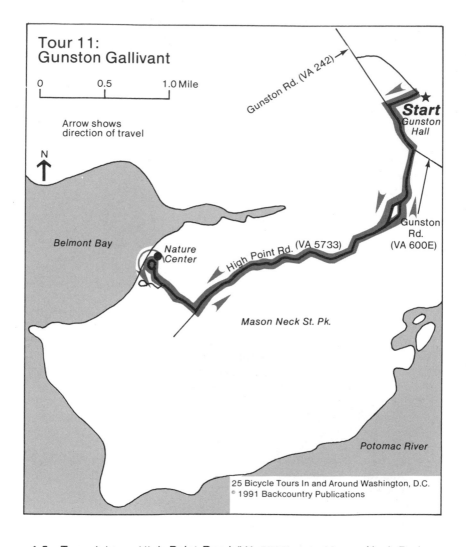

Tour 11:
Gunston Gallivant

0   0.5   1.0 Mile

Arrow shows
direction of travel

N

Gunston Rd. (VA 242)

★ Start
Gunston Hall

Gunston Rd.
(VA 600E)

Belmont Bay

Nature Center

High Point Rd. (VA 5733)

Mason Neck St. Pk.

Potomac River

25 Bicycle Tours In and Around Washington, D.C.
© 1991 Backcountry Publications

1.5 Turn right on High Point Road (VA 5733), into Mason Neck Park.
This is a lovely road that winds through a heavily wooded area and
curves along to the right.

4.5 The road ends at a nature center on the banks of Belmont Bay.
The nature center has a slide show and exhibits detailing the natural
history of the area, once prime hunting and fishing grounds for the
Dogue Indians. In the 19th and 20th century, loggers stripped the
area of much of the pine and hardwoods, which led to a decline in

Visitors are welcome to tour the 18th century mansion and gardens at Gunston Hall, home of colonial statesman George Mason.

the bald eagle population. Today, protection of the bald eagles— which have returned in encouraging numbers—is a prime purpose of the park. The fishermen have also returned, both in boats and along the shore. Here, you'll find a beach to walk along and miles of hiking trails. You can picnic on the wide lawn that overlooks Belmont Bay, an arm of the Potomac River.

After leaving the nature center area, double back on the park road.

7.5 Turn left on Gunston Road (VA 600W). The road makes a gradual climb.

8.4 Turn right into Gunston Hall.

9.0 Arrive back at the visitors' center parking lot.

Bicycle Repair Service
Bicycle Exchange, 7702 Gunston Plaza Drive, Lorton, Virginia (703-339-7300)

12.

Two Towns of the Past: Occoquan and Clifton

Location: Fairfax and Prince William Counties, Virginia
Terrain: Hilly
Road conditions: Paved roads, some with moderately heavy traffic
Distance: 29.8 miles
Highlights: The historic port of Occoquan, Lorton Reformatory, Fountainhead
   Regional Park, the landmark town of Clifton.

This tour links two historic towns that have escaped the suburbanization
of northern Virginia. Occoquan, once a bustling port and mill town on the
banks of the Occoquan River, now bustles with shops, restaurants, art

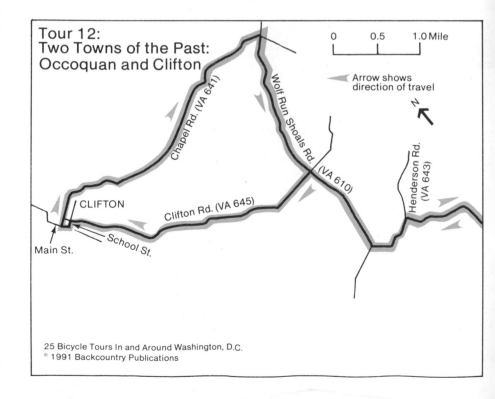

Tour 12:
Two Towns of the Past:
Occoquan and Clifton

0   0.5   1.0 Mile

Arrow shows
direction of travel

N

Chapel Rd. (VA 641)

Wolf Run Shoals Rd.

(VA 610)

Henderson Rd.
(VA 643)

CLIFTON

Clifton Rd. (VA 645)

School St.

Main St.

25 Bicycle Tours In and Around Washington, D.C.
© 1991 Backcountry Publications

and craft studios. The home of a fleet of pleasure boats, it bursts at the seams each September during a popular craft fair. Its name derives from an Indian word meaning "at the end of the water," and it stands near the point where the Occoquan River runs into the Potomac. The tour follows the river upstream, then goes north to Clifton, another town happily left behind by progress. Clifton is a former railroad center. Its tree-shaded streets hold 68 houses—homes for 200 residents. The entire town is on the National Register of Historic Places, and a sign in front of each building details its history.

Between historic towns, the tour skirts the forbidding Lorton Reformatory, a District of Columbia prison, and travels through both the encroaching suburbia and the surviving farmland of Fairfax County, as well as Fountainhead Regional Park on the Occoquan Reservoir.

The tour begins in Occoquan. To get there, take I-95 south from the Capital Beltway to exit 53. Take VA 123 north for .5 mile to the Occoquan turnoff on your left. Follow signs to the municipal parking lot. You will probably want to bike around the town before setting off on the tour. The

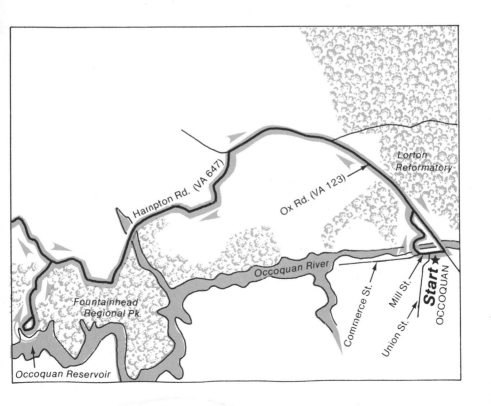

The town park in historic Clifton, Virginia, provides a peaceful picnic stop for cyclists.

Historic Occoquan Mill House Museum, on Commerce Street, is a good place to learn about Occoquan's past. This building served as the miller's office and is the only remaining part of the once-prosperous gristmill that was ravaged by fire in 1916. European activity in Occoquan began in 1736 when a tobacco warehouse was built. A few decades later, the town was an industrial center with sawmills and the country's first automated gristmill. Grain was taken off ships and barges, processed, then put back on board, ready to be shipped to markets as far away as the West Indies. By 1828 Occoquan also had a cotton mill, one of Virginia's first. Hotels and stores sprang up to serve the farmers, sailors, and traders who flocked here. In the 1850s a ship-building industry began in yards along the river. The river was also a source for ice, which was cut and shipped to Washington. The fire of 1916, plus the silting up of the river, began the town's decline. Hurricane Agnes, in 1972, just about completed it. But Occoquan rose again and now has more than 120 shops and restaurants in a compact area. The mileage count begins at Mill and Union Streets, in front of the Occoquan Inn. If you decide to have a meal there, be sure to check the bathroom on the second floor. The ghost of Occoquan's last Indian is said to make periodic appearances in the mirror.

0.0 Head up Union Street, away from the waterfront.

0.1 Turn left on Center Street.

0.3 Turn left on Ox Road (VA 123).
Watch for traffic on this road, which crosses the Occoquan River, climbs a hill, and passes the entrance to Occoquan Regional Park.

1.6 On your right is Lorton Reformatory, a correctional facility run by the District of Columbia. At the V, bear left, continuing on Ox Road.

3.3 Just past the farm stand on your right, turn left on Hampton Road (VA 647).
This is a quieter road that winds up and down hills, past large homes in wooded settings.

6.3 Turn left into Fountainhead Regional Park.

7.4 You'll find a small snack bar, as well as a dock and boat-rental concession. This makes a good rest and picnic stop and affords a view of the lake-like Occoquan Reservoir, formed by Ryans Dam, just upstream on the Occoquan River. This is a favorite spot for fishermen and for people who like to cruise the quiet waters to observe beavers and waterfowl.

8.5 After doubling back on the park road, turn left on Hampton Road.

9.9 Hampton Road ends. Turn left on Henderson Road (VA 643).

10.4 Turn right on Wolf Run Shoals Road (VA 610), a straightaway through farm fields.

11.6 Turn left on Clifton Road. Watch for traffic.
The road winds up and down hills then passes through a wooded area and descends into Clifton.

14.7 Turn left on School Street then right on Main Street, which is actually the continuation of Clifton Road.
Main Street has two restaurants, the Hermitage Inn (country French) and the Heart in Hand (southern). For a less formal meal, stop at the Clifton Store, which makes sandwiches to order, and have a picnic in the park behind the Baptist Church. The park has a playground, a long sloping lawn, picnic tables, and a gazebo. It is part of the legacy of Clifton's old-fashioned town planning. Most of the houses were built close to the street, with large common areas behind them. Unlike Occoquan, this is a largely residential town, but there are several antique and craft shops and a children's bookstore to browse through. The town dates from the 1850s when the Virginia Midland Railroad built a station here. The station was torn down in

the 1950s, but the stationmaster's house still stands along the railroad track, a short distance to the left down the dirt road just north of the Clifton Store. This house—like all the others—has a sign in front detailing its history. When the railroad stopped coming here, the town slept for a few decades. But young professionals looking for an alternative to the suburban lifestyle have revived—and preserved—Clifton.

From the Clifton store, go south on Main Street; then turn left on Chapel Road (VA 641).

18.2   Make a sharp right onto Wolf Run Shoals Road (VA 610).

21.1   Turn left on Henderson Road (VA 643).

22.4   Turn right on Hampton Road (VA 647).

26.5   Turn right on Ox Road (VA 123).

29.6   After crossing the Occoquan River on Ox Road, make a sharp right at the Occoquan turnoff.

29.8   Return to parking lot.

Bicycle Repair Service

The Bicycle Exchange, 7702 Gunston Plaza Drive, Lorton, Virginia (703-339-7300)

13.

Winding Your Way to Waterford

Location: Loudon County, Virginia
Terrain: Hilly
Road conditions: A paved bike trail, paved country roads, and an optional dirt-and-gravel road
Distance: 20.2 miles
Highlights: The Museum of the American Workhorse, the landmark Quaker village of Waterford, Morven Park, historic Leesburg.

Pennsylvania Quakers settled Waterford in 1733, but the town, nestled in the rolling hills between the Potomac River and the Blue Ridge Mountains, got its name a few years later when an Irish settler named Thomas Moore persuaded his neighbors to name the growing village after his hometown back in Ireland. Waterford served the surrounding farms, providing such services as milling, tanning, and coachmaking. The entire village is now a National Historic Landmark and presents a rare opportunity for visitors to see an intact 18th- and 19th-century village.

Although Waterford is the centerpiece of this tour, there are a lot of things to see en route, including the peaceful hamlet of Paeonian Springs with its museum dedicated to workhorses, and Morven Park, a Greek Revival mansion with a museum devoted to hounds and hunting. The trip begins in Leesburg, which was founded in 1758 and served as the nation's capital for a few days during the War of 1812. The Constitution and the Declaration of Independence were brought here at that time for safekeeping. Bicycle Outfitters, located two blocks from the W & OD Trail in downtown Leesburg, allows cyclists to use its parking lot as a starting point. If you have a large group or if the lot is full, ask at the bike shop for alternative parking suggestions. To get to Bicycle Outfitters from the Beltway, take VA 7 west to Leesburg. The shop is just off VA 7 at 19 Catoctin Circle. Mileage count starts at Catoctin Circle and the W & OD Trail.

0.0 Enter the W & OD Trail, heading west. The trail traverses suburban backyards at first, then heads into the country.

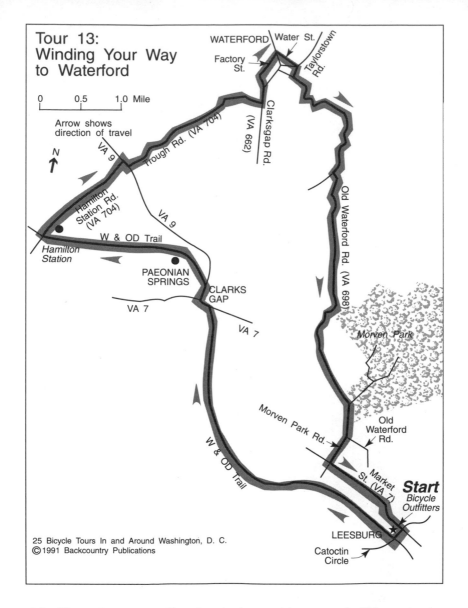

Tour 13:
Winding Your Way
to Waterford

WATERFORD Water St.

Factory St.

Taylorstown Rd.

0   0.5   1.0 Mile

Arrow shows
direction of travel

N

Clarksgap Rd.

(VA 662)

Trough Rd. (VA 704)

VA 9

Hamilton
Station Rd.
(VA 704)

VA 9

W & OD Trail

Hamilton
Station

PAEONIAN
SPRINGS

CLARKS
GAP

VA 7

VA 7

Old Waterford Rd. (VA 698)

Morven Park

Morven Park Rd.

Old
Waterford
Rd.

W & OD Trail

Market
St. (VA 7)

Start
Bicycle
Outfitters

LEESBURG

Catoctin
Circle

25 Bicycle Tours In and Around Washington, D. C.
©1991 Backcountry Publications

4.6   The trail passes under a hundred-year-old stone arch. This marks the
highest point on the trail at Clarks Gap. Just past the arch, the trail
goes through some convolutions to get riders safely across VA 7 and
VA 9. Follow trail markers.

5.5 On your left is the tiny Paeonian Springs Post Office, a good
jumping-off place for a tour of this pastoral village with its big, old
trees and white frame houses. A short ride up the street in front

of the post office is the Museum of the American Workhorse. It's open Wednesdays, April through October, or by appointment (703-338-6290). Even if the museum is closed, it's worth wandering by to catch a glimpse of Clydesdales grazing in the pasture.

7.4 At the defunct Hamilton Station (right), leave the trail and turn right on Hamilton Station Road (VA 704).

8.7 VA 704 crosses VA 9 and becomes Trough Road. This is a hilly but pleasant road, with a farm stand or two.

10.6 Turn left on Clarksgap Road (VA 662).

11.0 Turn left on Factory Street, which will lead you past picturesque homes and into the heart of Waterford.

The town has a lot of shops, including one grocery store, but no restaurants. Many of the historic homes are open for tours on one weekend in October. Contact the Waterford Foundation (703-882-3018) for information and for a map to use for walking tours, or pick one up at one of the shops. Of particular interest are the mill, the weaver's cottage, the tin shop, the Second Street School, and the jail.

If time and money permit, you can stay in one of the historic buildings that now offer bed and breakfast, including The Pink House (703-882-3453), The Waterford Inn (703-882-3465), and The James Moore House (703-882-3342).

The return trip to Leesburg uses a dirt-and-gravel road. It's rough going in places and you may have to walk your bike, but the views and absence of cars make it worth the trouble. If you prefer, however, you may return to Leesburg the way you came. To follow the tour, continue up Factory Street to the intersection with Water Street.

11.8 Turn right on Water Street, which becomes Taylorstown Road (VA 665).

12.2 In front of Waterford Elementary School, turn right on old Waterford Road (VA 698).

On your left is a stone building, now a private home, constructed as a Friends Meeting House in 1761.

11.8 The unpaved part of the road begins, winding mainly uphill past horse and cattle farms.

14.5 At the crossroads where Old Waterford Road meets Hurley Road (VA 703), continue on Old Waterford Road, bearing left.

Keep looking to your left for spectacular views of the Potomac River and the top of Sugarloaf Mountain on the Maryland side. Watch for

Bikes and horses share the Washington and Old Dominion Trail, built on an old railroad bed.

deer and hawks, too. Ride slowly, even downhill, to avoid getting caught in the gravel.

17.9 **The paved road begins.**

17.7 On your left is the entrance to Morven Park, which is open for tours weekends in May through October, and Tuesday through Sunday from Memorial Day through Labor Day. There is an admission fee. The mansion, originally a fieldstone farmhouse, has a Greek Revival portico, a Jacobean dining room, and a French drawing room. There are also exhibits on fox hunting and a collection of coaches. Picnic grounds are also available.

18.5 **Just past the entrance to the Marion Dupont Scott Equine Medical Center (left), Old Waterford Road turns left. Bear right on Morven Park Road.**

19.0 **Turn left on Market Street (VA 7). Watch for traffic.**

19.5 **Turn right on King Street.**

If you're hungry after your trip, the Georgetown Cafe on your right is recommended. The attached Colonial Inn offers lodging.

19.7 **Enter the W & OD Trail, heading east.**

20.2 **At Catoctin Circle, exit the trail and return to Bicycle Outfitters.**

Bicycle Repair Service
Bicycle Outfitters, 19 Catoctin Circle NE, Leesburg, Virginia, (703-777-6126)

14.

Sampling Virginia Vineyards

Location: Middleburg, Virginia, and environs
Terrain: Rolling hills
Road conditions: Mostly paved roads but some dirt and gravel roads; light traffic, but caution advised on narrow, winding stretches
Distance: 10.4 miles
Highlights: Chic, historic Middleburg, tasting and picnicking at two picturesque wineries.

Middleburg dates from 1731 when a cousin of George Washington opened a tavern on Ashby's Gap Turnpike. The turnpike is now known as US 50 and the tavern as the Red Fox. Today Middleburg is the site of multimillion-dollar horse farms and a few wineries. Horse farms welcome the public only once a year, usually Memorial Day weekend, in a stable tour that benefits Trinity Episcopal Church in nearby Upperville. Wineries offer their hospitality on a regular basis.

Find a parking space in the vicinity of the Red Fox Inn at US 50 and Madison Street or park in the inn's lot if you plan to eat there either before or after your tour. The mileage count begins at the intersection of US 50 and VA 626 (The Plains Road), one block west of the Red Fox.

0.0 From US 50 turn left (south) onto VA 626.
You'll climb and descend some hills and pass large estates with horse pastures protected by stone fences.

2.8 Turn right into Piedmont Vineyards and Winery.
Pass the sign requesting "Do Not Bother Swans" and the mellow, yellow Waverly, a landmark pre–Revolutionary War mansion and residence of the Furness family, which founded the vineyard in 1973. Although Virginians, including Thomas Jefferson, had long sought to establish wineries, this was the first commercial vinifera vineyard in the state. The 36-acre vineyard is planted with Chardonnay, Semillon, and Seyval Blanc grapes.

3.0 Park at the old dairy barn that now houses the winery and sales room,

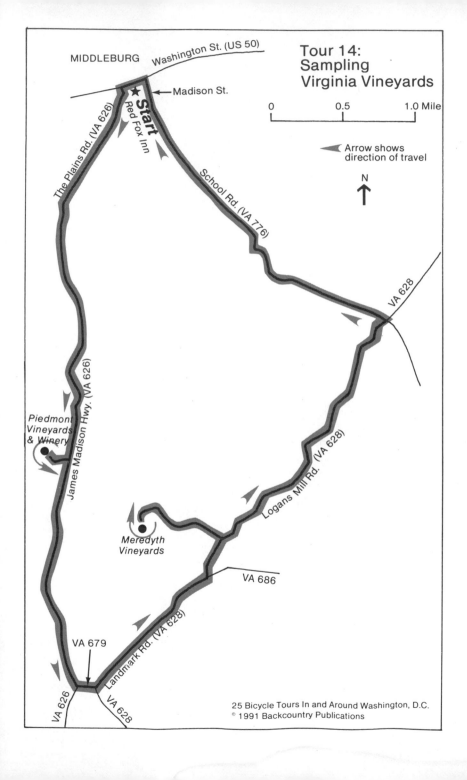

MIDDLEBURG Washington St. (US 50)

Tour 14:
Sampling
Virginia Vineyards

← Madison St.

0   0.5   1.0 Mile

◄ Arrow shows
direction of travel

N
↑

The Plains Rd. (VA 626)

Red Fox Inn

Start

School Rd. (VA 776)

VA 628

James Madison Hwy. (VA 626)

Piedmont
Vineyards
& Winery

Logans Mill Rd. (VA 628)

Meredyth
Vineyards

VA 686

VA 679

Landmark Rd. (VA 628)

VA 626

VA 628

25 Bicycle Tours In and Around Washington, D.C.
© 1991 Backcountry Publications

Workers harvest grapes at Meredyth Vineyards. The picturesque ruins in the background make intriguing settings for picnics.

open Tuesday through Sunday 10 a.m. to 4 p.m. Tours and tastings are informal and free.

A guide will walk you through the wine-making process and show you the machines that press the grapes, the stainless steel tanks where the juice, or "must," is placed in order to allow the suspended solid matter to settle out, and the temperature-controlled oak fermenting barrels. Piedmont produces about 7,000 cases of wine a year. The output includes two Chardonnays, a Semillon, and two white wines made from the Seyal Blanc grape. Little River White is semidry, and Hunt Country White is dry. You'll be invited to taste several wines, and you'll probably want to buy a bottle for your picnic. Since biking and drinking aren't compatible, go easy on the tasting. Just outside the winery are picnic tables. As you picnic with Waverly as a backdrop, don't be surprised to have horses looking over your shoulder.

After the tour, continue south on VA 626.

3.4   Turn left on VA 679 (not well marked, easy to miss).

3.5   VA 679 ends. Bear left on VA 628.

4.6   VA 628 meets VA 686 at a "V." Bear left, remaining on VA 628.

4.9   Take a left at the Meredyth Vineyards sign and follow the dirt road that leads through the 56-acre vineyard, set against the spectacular backdrop of the Bull Run Mountains.
        On your way in, you'll come to some picturesque picnic grounds, complete with ruins of old stone buildings, but you may want to wait until you've taken the tour and purchased some wine.

5.3   Park in front of the winery, a large green barn.
        Tours are available daily 10 a.m. to 4 p.m. (except Christmas, Easter, Thanksgiving, and New Year's Day). Meredyth produces an impressive variety of wines, including Seyval Blanc, Villard Blanc, Riesling, Chardonnay, Cabernet Sauvignon, and Merlot, from its French-American hybrids, and the winery puts on a good tour. Go easy on the tasting.

5.7   Exit the vineyard and go left on VA 628.
        The road is loosely packed gravel with lots of hills.

7.7   Turn left on VA 776. This becomes Madison Street in Middleburg.

10.3   Arrive back at the intersection of Madison Street and US 50.
        You've probably earned a good feed at either the Red Fox Inn or its less formal appendage, Mosby's Tavern, named for Confederate irregular John Mosby who operated in these parts. You may also want to window shop or even spend money in Middleburg's chic boutiques, antique shops, galleries, and gunshops, which line Route 50, Madison Street, and nearby side streets.

Bicycle Repair Service
Bicycle Outfitters, 19 Catoctin Circle NE, Leesburg, Virginia, (703-777-6126)

15.

By the Old Mill Stream

Location: The Shenandoah Valley of Virginia (Clarke County)
Terrain: Roller-coaster hills with some flat stretches
Road conditions: Light traffic on paved roads
Distance: 27.7 miles
Highlights: The restored Burwell-Morgan Mill, antique shops, the Shenandoah River.

This tour is especially fun in the summer, since, after you've mastered the roller-coaster hills, you can cool off in the clean, fresh Shenandoah. (Because there's no place to change, you might want to wear a swimsuit under your clothes). In the shadow of the Blue Ridge, this is apple, horse, and cattle country, with hilly farms marked off by stone fences. Except during hunting season, you're likely to spot some deer.

The tour begins in Millwood, an 18th-century town with lovely old homes, a restored and working mill, and several antique shops. To reach Millwood, take I-66 west to US 17 north. Follow US 17 to the intersection with US 50. Take US 50 west. Just after you cross the Shenandoah River, turn right onto VA 723. The Burwell-Morgan Mill is on your left in Millwood. Park in the parking lot.

0.0 After visiting the mill, exit the parking lot and turn right onto VA 723. The Burwell-Morgan Mill, completed in 1785 by two men who met serving in the Revolutionary War, once served the local wheat-growing community. Today it serves picnickers and history buffs and grinds and sells corn meal. During the Civil War, troops from both armies bought flour—and swapped yarns—here. It ceased operations in 1953 and was later restored by the Clarke County Historical Association. A small donation is requested for a tour of the 40-by-60-foot building with an indoor overshot waterwheel, wooden gears, and French grindstones. Barrels of flour were once stored in the building until the waters of the Shenandoah were high enough to float them in flat boats to Harpers Ferry. (See tour 25.) From there they were put on canal boats bound for Georgetown. (You can buy the mill's corn meal in small bags, each imprinted with a picture of

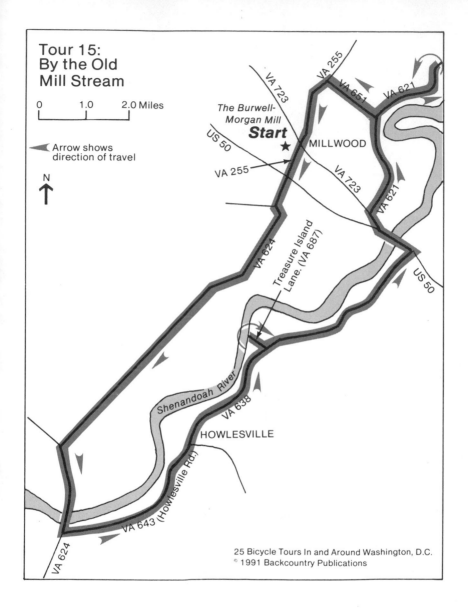

Tour 15:
By the Old
Mill Stream

0   1.0   2.0 Miles

◀ Arrow shows
   direction of travel

N
↑

The Burwell-
Morgan Mill
Start
★

MILLWOOD

VA 255

VA 723

VA 651

VA 621

US 50

VA 255

VA 723

VA 621

US 50

VA 624

Treasure Island
Lane. (VA 687)

Shenandoah River

VA 638

HOWLESVILLE

VA 643 (Howlesville Rd.)

VA 624

25 Bicycle Tours In and Around Washington, D.C.
© 1991 Backcountry Publications

the building.) The mill uses the waters of Spout Run, which is lined with willows that shelter several picnic tables on the lush green. Adjacent to the mill is Brookside Bed and Breakfast and Antiques, built in 1780. Several more antique shops are within walking distance.

0.2   Turn right on VA 255.

0.8   Cross US 50 carefully. On the other side of US 50, the road becomes VA 624. Follow it through the intersection with VA 622.

This stretch of road consists of roller-coaster hills through farm country, with mountains on your right side and hills sloping down toward the river on your left.

7.7   VA 624 turns left for an enjoyable and well-earned downhill run to the river.

9.0   Cross the wide Shenandoah on a low, narrow bridge. Continue on VA 624, climbing uphill slightly.

You will probably see cows wading in the river. On the other side of the river there's a boat launch, and this is a very popular fishing spot. You could wade or swim here, but there's a better spot farther along.

9.3   Turn left on VA 643, Howlesville Road. After passing through the small settlement of Howlesville, VA 643 becomes VA 638.

This road is less picturesque, but also less hilly, than the road on the other side of the river.

15.2   Turn left on VA 687, Treasure Island Lane, a suburban-like street that ends in a cul-de-sac at 15.4.

Lock your bike to a tree or push it along the dirt patch down to a tributary of the river. A defunct and deteriorating pedestrian bridge hangs over the water in a cool, green Corot-like glade. You can picnic or wade here, but for deeper, wider water, follow the stream to your right, walking in the water for about a quarter of a mile to the intersection with the Shenandoah. This is a great spot for a swim and, since there's no road access, it definitely won't be crowded. After lingering here as long as time allows, return to your bike and double back up Treasure Island Lane.

15.6   Turn left on VA 638.

16.6 You'll find a grocery store on your right.

19.8   Cross US 50 and turn left. Ride on the shoulder across the Shenandoah.

20.3   Take a right on VA 723 and an immediate right again on VA 621.

This is a scenic country road that winds through farm country, up and down small hills. Watch for deer in the fields.

23.6   At the intersection with VA 651, VA 621 continues as a dirt road along the river. If you want to take another swim, follow it for a few hundred yards. To continue the tour, turn left at the intersection onto VA 651, which climbs a medium-sized hill.

25.4   Turn left on VA 255.

Whether you're traveling on four legs or two wheels, a dip in the Shenandoah offers a refreshing respite.

26.6 On your left, private but visible from the road, stands Carter Hall, a stone manor house built by Lieutenant Colonel Nathaniel Burwell, one of the owners of the Burwell-Morgan Mill. The house was built in 1792 and named for Burwell's former home, Carter's Grove, one of the famous James River plantations. In 1862 Stonewall Jackson set up headquarters here but refused an invitation to stay in the house. Instead, he camped on the lawn with his troops. Across the road is Christ Episcopal Church, which dates from 1832. Lovely old homes — some modest, some grand — line the road as it approaches Millwood.

27.6 Just before the intersection with VA 723 you will see an old red schoolhouse, built in 1858, that now houses an antique store.

27.6 Turn left onto 723.

27.7 Turn right into the mill parking lot.

Bicycle Repair Service
Winchester Bicycle Center, 711 Baker Knight Street, Winchester, Virginia, (703-662-5744)

Maryland Tours

16.

Two Wheels around Takoma

Location: The District and Maryland's Montgomery County and Prince George's County
Terrain: Flat to moderately hilly
Road conditions: Paved bike trails and suburban streets, some with moderately heavy traffic
Distance: 12.6 miles
Highlights: Takoma Park, Northwest Branch Park, Adelphi Mill.

In the 1880s, a developer named Ben Gilbert founded Washington's first railroad suburb and christened it Takoma. The Baltimore and Ohio Railroad transported residents between downtown and Takoma's pleasant Victorian houses with their wraparound porches. Today, Metro runs along the old B & O tracks to Takoma, and the town is enjoying a revival. It guards against "yuppification," however, by clinging to a distinctly 1960s aura, evidenced by a bead shop, an annual folk music festival, and a bike path named after a guru. There are actually two Takomas — the Takoma neighborhood of the District of Columbia and Takoma Park, Maryland. They are contiguous and architecturally similar, with frame Victorian houses and bungalows along quiet streets shaded by old trees. This tour begins at the Takoma Metro station, which is in D.C., and then enters the Takoma Park Historic District in Maryland. After a peaceful ride along the Sri Chinmoy Peace Mile and a not-so-peaceful ride along Piney Branch Road, the tour picks up another off-road bike path that follows the Northwest Branch of the Anacostia River and visits Adelphi Mill. The tour loops around, through acres of apartment houses and pleasant suburban neighborhoods, back to Takoma Park. After a ride through the attractively funky business district and a stop at the Sunday farmers market, the tour returns to the Takoma Metro station.

0.0 Exit the Takoma station on the west side and turn right on Eastern Avenue.

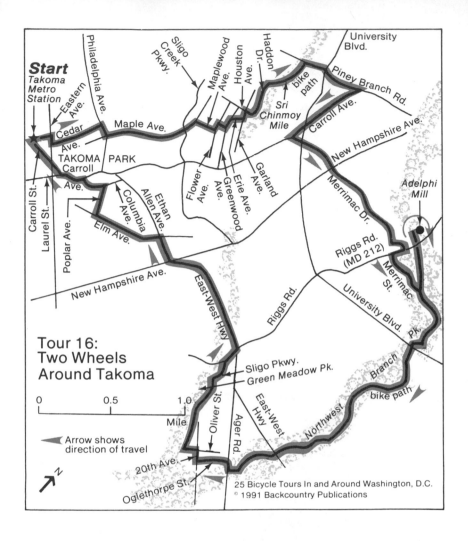

Tour 16:
Two Wheels
Around Takoma

0   0.5   1.0

Mile

◄ Arrow shows
direction of travel

25 Bicycle Tours In and Around Washington, D.C.
© 1991 Backcountry Publications

0.1 Turn left on Cedar Avenue, an encyclopedia of architectural styles from Queen Anne to stick style to bungalows. Watch for speed bumps.

0.5 Cedar Avenue ends at Philadelphia Avenue. Turn right on Philadelphia Avenue and left again on Maple Avenue, which traverses an area of apartment buildings then crosses Sligo Creek Parkway and climbs a hill past the Washington Adventist Hospital.

1.1 Turn right on Maplewood Avenue, which jogs left, crosses Flower Avenue, and continues to Greenwood Avenue.

1.4 Turn left on Greenwood Avenue then right on Erie Avenue.

1.6 Turn left on Garland Avenue then right on Houston Avenue to Haddon Drive, which follows a green park along a stream.

1.8 Bear right on a bike path through a green park along Long Branch. Signs label this part of the trail the Sri Chinmoy Peace Mile in honor of a mystic who led a march here.

2.1 The trail crosses a footbridge and continues on the opposite side of the stream.

This is a green, wooded trail bounded by back yards on one side and the stream on the other.

2.3 The trail ends at Piney Branch Road. Turn right, watching for traffic. Piney Branch crosses University Avenue (MD 193) then goes down a long hill.

2.8 Turn right on Carroll Avenue, which goes uphill, past the garden apartments that characterize the Langley Park community.

3.3 Carroll Avenue crosses University Avenue. Right after you cross University Avenue, turn left on Merrimac Drive, walking your bike across New Hampshire Avenue and picking up Merrimac Drive again on the other side.

4.5 Merrimac Drive, now a quiet street lined with small homes, jogs left and meets Riggs Road (MD 212).

4.6 Turn right on Riggs Road then make an immediate left on Merrimac Street.

4.8 Merrimac Street ends. Continue on the grass right of way, straight ahead to the bike path in Northwest Branch Park. Turn left by the small park building and follow the path across a footbridge.

You may see retrievers being trained in the creek below you. The trail follows the creek through a wooded area.

5.3 The stone cottage on your right once housed the miller who ran Adelphi Mill, which is reached by continuing on the trail about a hundred feet and crossing under Riggs Road. The mill, which dates from 1796, started out as a gristmill and later housed a wool-carding operation. Picnic tables and large shade trees make this a good place to visit, maybe wade.

After your visit, reverse direction on the trail.

6.6 At the intersection of the trail and University Avenue, in a small shopping center on the right, is the Loch Lomond Bakery, which offers freshly baked scones and other Scottish specialties. Cross University Avenue at the light and continue on the trail. On your left, just after the intersection, is a public outdoor swimming pool. This part of the park also contains picnic tables on wide lawns.

8.8 The bike path ends at Ager Road. Cross Ager Road and continue in the same direction on Oglethrope Street, between blocks of garden apartments.

9.0 Turn right on 20th Street.

9.1 Turn left on Oliver Street.

9.2 Turn right on Sligo Parkway.
This is a quiet street with Green Meadow Park on one side and small, neat houses on the other.

Takoma Park, Maryland, Washington's first railroad suburb, hosts an outdoor produce and craft market every Sunday.

9.9 Sligo Parkway ends at the very busy intersection of Riggs Road and East-West Highway (MD 410). Cross Riggs Road and then cross East-West Highway. Turn left on East-West Highway, using the frontage road. Where the frontage road ends, a sidewalk begins.

In places, the sidewalk is separated from the road by shrubbery and makes a pleasant bike path, crossing Sligo Creek on a footbridge.

10.9 After crossing New Hampshire Avenue, East-West Highway becomes Ethan Allen Avenue. Continue on Ethan Allen Avenue for a short distance.

11.0 Turn left on Elm Avenue, which runs through a hilly neighborhood.

11.5 At the intersection of Elm and Poplar, there's a small park with a water fountain. Turn right on Poplar Avenue, reentering the Takoma Park Historic District.

This is a picture-book block with old homes set back from the street. Note the pagoda-like roof on the house at 7009 Poplar Avenue.

11.8 Turn left on Columbia Avenue on one of the biggest hills of this tour.

12.0 Turn left on Carroll Avenue, the main street of downtown Takoma Park.

A microcosm of the town's character, it's lined with antique shops, book shops, cafes — even a bead shop. The House of Musical Traditions, which features handmade instruments, is especially worth a visit.

12.2 Carroll Avenue turns to the right and becomes Carroll Street. Continue on Carroll Street.

If you went straight ahead you would be on Laurel Avenue. On Sundays, this part of Laurel Avenue turns into a street market, with organic produce, baked goods, and crafts for sale.

12.6 Turn right into the Takoma Metro station.

Bicycle Repair Service

Griffin Cycle, Inc., 12848 New Hampshire Ave., Silver Spring, Maryland, (301-384-2111)

Proteus Bicycle and Fitness Shop, 9217 Baltimore Boulevard, College Park, Maryland, (301-441-2929)

17.

Triadelphia Trek

Location: Montgomery and Howard Counties in Maryland
Terrain: Moderately hilly to hilly
Road conditions: Light traffic except for short rides on roads with heavy traffic, paved roads and some optional dirt roads
Distance: 44 miles
Highlights: Historic Brookeville, Catoctin Vineyards, Triadelphia Reservoir, Brighton Dam.

Brighton Dam dams up the Patuxent River to create Triadelphia Reservoir, a major source of water for 1.3 million people in Montgomery and Prince George's County. The Triadelphia watershed area also provides superb recreation and scenery. It's a mecca for fishermen and nonpower boaters, and also affords good picnic spots and places for people who want to get away from the hustle and bustle of the metropolis. There are no bike trails and no road that hugs the shoreline, but it's possible to ride across the dam and around the reservoir on low-traffic roads with side trips for rests, picnics, and views of the water.

The trip starts at the Shady Grove station, about as far into the country as Metro will take you. In a short time after exiting the Metro station, you'll be in the country—although you'll never be far from encroaching development. Country roads will lead you through wooded areas, past small farms and babbling brooks to lovely, leafy Brookeville, a 19th-century town where people sit on wide front porches and watch the passing parade.

After a stop at Catoctin Vineyard, the closest winery to Washington, you'll be at the reservoir's edge. Please remember that swimming and wading are prohibited. (If you must wade, there's an inviting stretch of the Patuxent farther on.) Also remember that bike helmets are required by law for children 16 or under in both Howard and Montgomery counties.

0.0 Exit the Shady Grove Metro station by the bus route and turn left on Redlands Road.

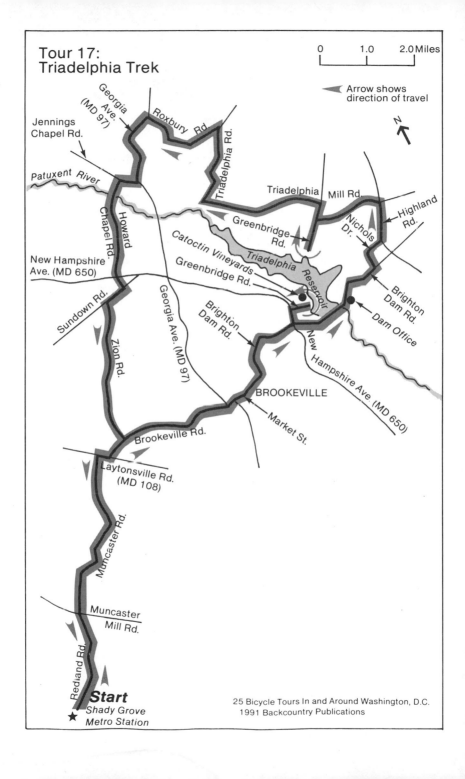

Tour 17:
Triadelphia Trek

0   1.0   2.0 Miles

Arrow shows direction of travel

N

Georgia Ave. (MD 97)

Roxbury Rd.

Jennings Chapel Rd.

Triadelphia Rd.

Patuxent River

Triadelphia Mill Rd.

Highland Rd.

Greenbridge Rd.

Nichols Dr.

Howard Chapel Rd.

Catoctin Vineyards

Triadelphia Reservoir

New Hampshire Ave. (MD 650)

Greenbridge Rd.

Brighton Dam Rd.

Sundown Rd.

Georgia Ave. (MD 97)

Brighton Dam Rd.

Dam Office

Zion Rd.

New Hampshire Ave. (MD 650)

BROOKEVILLE

Market St.

Brookeville Rd.

Laytonsville Rd. (MD 108)

Muncaster Rd.

Muncaster Mill Rd.

Redland Rd.

Start
Shady Grove Metro Station

25 Bicycle Tours In and Around Washington, D.C.
1991 Backcountry Publications

2.8   Cross Muncaster Mill Road. (You'll find fast food, stores, and gas stations.) Redlands Road continues as Muncaster Road.

6.7   Muncaster Road ends. Turn right on Laytonsville Road (MD 108).
George's Liquor Store (right) has carry-out food.

6.8   Taking care to avoid the traffic on Laytonsville Road, turn left onto Brookeville Road.
This is a pleasant, three-mile stretch past farms and woods.

9.8   Brookeville Road ends at Georgia Avenue (MD 97). Bear right on Georgia Avenue and follow it as it winds up a hill, past grand but unpretentious houses into the town of Brookeville.

10.0 At the top of the hill stands the post office (right). After the British burned the White House, James and Dolly Madison found refuge near here on August 26, 1814, in the home of Brookeville postmaster Caleb Bently.

10.0   Georgia Avenue turns right in front of the post office. The tour goes straight, past the side of the post office, on Market Street. Market Street takes you past more lovely homes and, at the bottom of a hill, leaves town and becomes Brighton Dam Road, which rolls up and down hills.

12.7   Turn left on New Hampshire Avenue (MD 650).
This is not a major artery at this point, but watch for traffic.

13.1   Turn right onto Greenbridge Road.
Watch immediately on your left for the entrance to Catoctin Vineyards. Tours are available on weekends from 12 to 5 p.m. (301-774-2310).

13.7   Enter the parking lot of the public boat launch and mooring facility.
Although there are no picnic tables, this is a great spot to rest and view the reservoir. When you've drunk in your fill of the scenery, double back to New Hampshire Avenue.

14.3   Turn left on New Hampshire Avenue.

14.7   Turn left on Brighton Dam Road, which is a series of roller-coaster hills.

15.9   Turn right into the parking lot of the Brighton Dam office and information center, which has exhibits about the dam and surrounding area.
At the end of the parking lot is a soda machine. Steps lead down to a picnic area in the midst of lush, inviting lawns below the dam. There is a playground and room to fish and walk along the Patuxent River. Across Brighton Dam Road, along the part of the reservoir that spills

into the dam, are some azalea gardens developed by dam employees. They are open daily from 12 to 7 p.m. during blooming season.

After a respite, continue on Brighton Dam Road across the dam. Once across, the road begins a steady climb.

17.0 Turn left on Nichols Drive.

18.1 Turn left on Highland Road.

19.0 Turn left on Triadelphia Mill Road.

This is an area of rolling hills and encroaching suburbia, with a few farm holdouts.

20.2 At the bottom of a hill, Triadelphia Mill Road runs into Greenbridge Road. For a rest by the reservoir, turn left on Greenbridge Road, which soon turns into easily negotiable, hard-packed gravel.

20.6 You'll arrive at the Pig Tail boat-launching area, where the water juts into the land in the shape of a pig's tail.

This is a nice place to sit under the weeping willows that grow along the bank.

Double back on the same road and continue on the paved portion of Greenbridge Road.

21.1 Turn left on Triadelphia Mill Road.

22.8 On the left side of the road is a pleasant picnic and boat-launch facility — your last chance to rest by the reservoir on this tour.

23.5 Triadelphia Mill Road ends. Turn right on Triadelphia Road.

25.2 Make a sharp left onto Roxbury Road, a rural road lined by cornfields.

27.5 Cross Georgia Avenue (MD 97) carefully and turn left, riding on the paved shoulder. Watch for traffic.

29.6 Turn right on Jennings Chapel Road.

29.9 Turn left on Howard Chapel Road.

This is a scenic and quiet road that runs through undeveloped parkland along the Patuxent River, which is really just a stream at this point. Watch for turtles crossing and for low-flying goldfinches.

30.4 The road crosses the Patuxent and reenters Montgomery County.

The point where the road crosses the stream is a good fishing, wading, and resting spot. Then the road goes up a slight incline past a horse farm.

32.2 Cross MD 650.

The Madisons would probably still recognize peaceful Brookeville, Maryland, whose quiet streets are lined with nineteenth century homes.

32.4   Turn right on Sundown Road. Watch for traffic.

32.9   Turn left on Zion Road.
This is a low-traffic road that leads past Mount Zion Church.

35.9   Turn right on Brookeville Road. From now on, you'll be retracing the route you took at the beginning of the trip.

36.5   Turn right on Laytonsville Road (MD 108).

36.6   Turn left on Muncaster Road.

39.0 On a hill to your right stands the Magruder Farm, owned by the county and used to teach schoolchildren about the county's agricultural past. It started as a tobacco farm in 1734 and later became a wheat farm known as Waveland.

41.7   Cross Muncaster Mill Road. Muncaster Road continues as Redland Road.
By this time you may be ready for some of the fast food available at this intersection.

44.0   Turn right into the Shady Grove Metro station parking lot.

Bicycle Repair Service
Gaithersburg Schwinn, 12 East Diamond Avenue, Gaithersburg, Maryland, (301-948-4407)

18.

Cruising around Croom

Location: Prince George's County, Maryland
Terrain: Almost flat
Road conditions: Park roads and country roads with light traffic
Distance: 28.5 miles
Highlights: Patuxent River Park, Merkle Wildlife Sanctuary, St. Thomas Church.

This tour takes you to a part of Prince George's County that's still country — a place where tobacco still grows, osprey still nest, and where the Canada geese come to eat the wild rice and end up staying for the winter. The tour begins at Patuxent River Park, where the Patuxent River widens into Jug Bay. Following the Chesapeake Bay Critical Areas Drive, the tour visits the first airfield in the United States owned and operated by a black and stops at an observation tower over a tidal marsh. After a stop at St. Thomas Church, completed in 1745, the tour takes in Merkle Wildlife Sanctuary and Visitor Center, which hosts hummingbirds and Canada geese, and continues to now-nonexistent Nottingham, a hotbed of intrigue and activity during the War of 1812. After a look at Mattaponi, built in 1745 by the Bowie family, the trip ends back in Patuxent River Park.

To get to Patuxent River Park from the Beltway, take MD 4 to US 301 south. Take US 301 to Croom Road (MD 382). Take Croom Road south to Croom Airport Road. Turn left on Croom Airport Road and continue to the park entrance. Park in the lot near the park office.

Either before or after your bike ride, you'll want to enjoy some of the attractions of this 2,000-acre park — by taking a walk on the boardwalk that leads through the wetlands and by touring the Patuxent Village, an exhibit that depicts life on the river in the 19th century. Check at the park office for a schedule of events. By calling ahead (301-627-6094), you may be able to make arrangements for canoeing or camping or for a ride on an electric boat.

0.0 Exit the parking lot and head back out the park road.

1.7 Turn left on Croom Airport Road, which winds to the left down a hill.

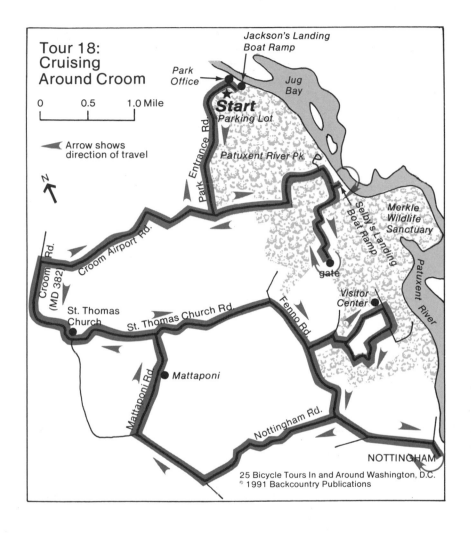

Tour 18: Cruising Around Croom

Jackson's Landing Boat Ramp

Park Office

Jug Bay

Start Parking Lot

Patuxent River Pk.

Merkle Wildlife Sanctuary

Selby's Landing Boat Ramp

Park Entrance Rd.

Croom Airport Rd.

Croom Rd. (MD 382)

St. Thomas Church

St. Thomas Church Rd.

Fenno Rd.

gate

Visitor Center

Patuxent River

Mattaponi Rd.

Mattaponi

Nottingham Rd.

NOTTINGHAM

0   0.5   1.0 Mile

Arrow shows direction of travel

N

25 Bicycle Tours In and Around Washington, D.C.
© 1991 Backcountry Publications

2.4 At the bottom of the hill, turn left, following the signs for Selby's Landing Boat Ramp.

3.1 A sign in a field marks the site of the Columbia Air Center, the first airfield owned and operated by a black. It was opened in 1941 by John W. Greene, Jr. During World War II, the Navy used the field for training.

3.7 Selby's Landing Boat Ramp has a dock if you want to sit by the river. Beyond the landing, the road, part of the Chesapeake Bay Critical Areas Drive, is open to cars only on Sunday afternoons. It winds through a wooded area.

4.8   **The road turns to a wooden bridge over a fresh water tidal marsh.**
An observation tower allows you to watch for the birds, muskrats, and diamondback terrapin that frequent the marsh. Serious bird watchers sometimes set up telescopes on the bridge. They appreciate quiet. On the other side of the bridge is Merkle Wildlife Sanctuary. Dirt roads lead to the visitors' center, but bicycles are not allowed on them except during supervised trips. Call 301-888-1410 to find out about these. Cars are allowed on the dirt roads on Sunday afternoons, the rationale being that wildlife are less intimidated by cars than by people they can see on bicycles. So, you need to backtrack to the entrance of Patuxent River Park on Croom Airport Road.

7.9   **At the park entrance continue on Croom Airport Road.**

9.9   **Turn left on Croom Road.**

10.3 The Country Corner Market stands on your right.

10.8   **Turn left on St. Thomas Church Road.**
On your left, immediately after the turn, is the church, completed in 1745 but with Victorian alterations. In the churchyard, among the pines and cedars, are graves of some of the first families of Maryland: Bowies and Calverts and Duvalls. There is also a memorial to a former rector, Thomas John Claggett, who later became the first Episcopalian Bishop consecrated in the United States. Inscribed on the memorial is a quote from Claggett: "How awesome is the dawn sky over the hills of Croom. . . It makes my heart sing 'praised be God.' "

13.2   **Turn right on Fenno Road.**
This is a rural road that parallels the river.

13.9   **Turn left into Merkle Wildlife Sanctuary and follow the one-way loop to the visitors' center.**
Merkle was a local farmer and wildlife lover who donated this property for conservation purposes. The center is open 10 a.m. to 4 p.m. Tuesday through Sunday and has exhibits on the river and the animals found in its watershed. A special feature is a hummingbird garden with telescopes set up so you can view the tiny birds at close range. There is also a pond favored by visiting waterfowl.

After your visit, return to Fenno Road, completing the one-way loop.

Cyclists rest beside the Patuxent River near Croom.

15.7 Turn left on Fenno Road.

17.6 Turn left on Nottingham Road. This road ends at the river, but with no access.

> Nottingham, which now consists of only a few houses, was once a thriving port. During the war of 1812, it served as headquarters for Commodore Joshua Barney, whose flotilla was bottled up here by the British fleet. Secretary of State James Monroe reportedly donned cloak and dagger and came to Nottingham to size up the British forces, who were advancing up the Patuxent and who camped in Nottingham the night of August 21, 1814.
>
> **Turn around and backtrack on Nottingham Road, continuing past the intersection with Fenno Road, through tobacco-farming country.**

20.7   Turn right on Croom Road (MD 382).

21.6   Turn right on Mattaponi Road.

>   22.3 Mattoponi (right), a two-and-a-half story hip-roofed house built about 1745, was once the ancestral home of the Bowies, some of whom are buried in St. Thomas churchyard. Today, it's owned by the Catholic Church.

22.8   Turn left on St. Thomas Church Road and follow it up a small hill, past the church.

23.7   Turn right on Croom Road.

24.8   Turn right on Croom Airport Road.

26.8   Turn left into Patuxent River Park.

28.5   Return to the parking lot.

Bicycle Repair Service
Clinton Bicycle, 8935 Woodyard Road, Clinton, Maryland, (301-868-0033)

19.

Getaway to Galesville

Location: Prince George's and Anne Arundel Counties in Maryland
Terrain: Rolling to moderately hilly
Road conditions: Paved roads, most with little traffic
Distance: 51.4 miles
Highlights: Historic churches; the Old Quaker Burying Ground; Galesville, with its restaurants, antique shops, and waterfront parks.

Galesville, long a popular boating destination for Washingtonians, also makes a good bike trip destination. It's probably the nearest Chesapeake Bay town to Washington—although it's actually on the West River near the point where the river joins the bay.

Galesville, established in 1684, was an active port during the steamboat era. Today Galesville is a stately old town with large frame houses lining the main street. Its economy is based on an oyster cannery, plus a lot of businesses that serve visiting boaters, including marinas and restaurants. What makes the town a nice place to visit is that some of its waterfront has been set aside as parkland, making it available for picnicking.

The tour starts at the New Carrollton Metro station, terminus of the Orange Line, and quickly takes the rider into the country.

0.0 Exit the New Carrollton station on the east side, following the bus lane. At the exit, turn right onto Garden City Drive, then left at the V, under US 50. Continue to the left on Ardwick Ardmore Road.

At first the road is lined with factories and other light industries, but it soon turns more country-like.

3.3 Ardwick Ardmore Road ends in front of the Enterprise Golf Club. Turn right on Lottsford Vista Road.

4.5 Lottsford Vista Road ends. Turn left on Lottsford Road.

5.2 Lottsford Road ends at Enterprise Road (MD 556). Cross Enterprise Road—carefully—and continue straight ahead on Woodmore Road.

5.7 The white clapboard Holy Family Catholic Church, set amidst tall trees, dates from 1890.

8.1 Woodmore Road ends at Church Road. On your right is the Mount Oak Methodist Church Cemetery, established in 1890. Turn left on Church Road; then make an immediate right onto Mount Oak Road.

> On your left just after the turn, is the Mount Oak Methodist Church, built in 1881. The road continues over rolling hills in a country setting.

9.8 Turn right on Mitchellville Road after stopping at the shopping center at the intersection for food if desired.

> You have reentered suburbia, the greater Bowie area.

11.1 Proceed carefully across US 301 and its large center island. At the other side of the highway, Mitchellville Road becomes Queen Anne Bridge Road.

> After a brief uphill climb, the road rolls through a pleasant rural area.

13.2 Turn left on Central Avenue (MD 214). Watch for traffic. After crossing the Patuxent River, you'll enter Anne Arundel County.

14.5 Turn right on Patuxent River Road in front of Sweet Mama's Home Cooked Food, which offers carry-out service.

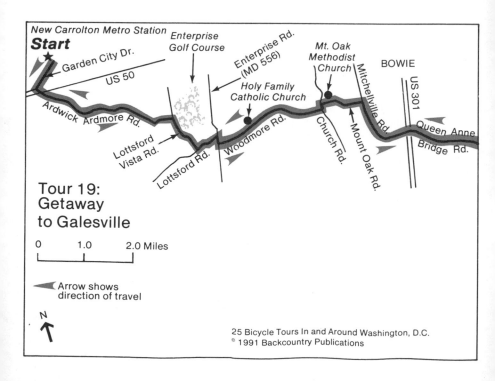

Tour 19:
Getaway
to Galesville

0   1.0   2.0 Miles

◄ Arrow shows
  direction of travel

N

25 Bicycle Tours In and Around Washington, D.C.
© 1991 Backcountry Publications

15.4 Turn left on Queen Anne Bridge Road.

16.6 Make a sharp right onto Wayson Road in front of the National Guard installation.

This stretch features roller-coaster hills.

17.9 Turn left on Harwood Road, which runs through cornfields and crosses shady Stocketts Run.

20.3 Cross Solomons Island Road (MD 2) at Harwood Post Office. Enter Old Solomons Island Road.

This is a rural loop that will minimize the time you have to spend on busy MD 2.

20.8 Old Solomons Island Road ends. Turn left onto Solomons Island Road. Ride on the shoulder.

21.0 Turn left on Owensville Sudley Road, which soon makes a right turn and travels through farm country.

22.3 Turn left on Owensville Road (MD 255).

Christ Church Parish Hall, at the intersection, has a big front yard

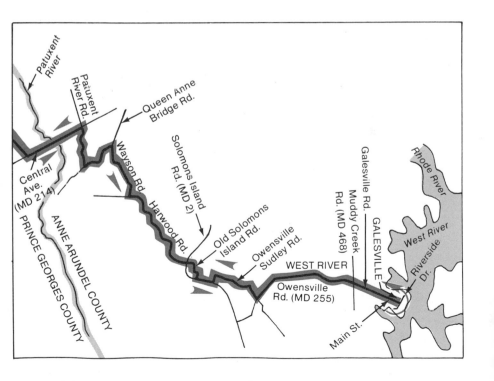

with a towering oak to rest under. Next door is the Episcopal church itself, a white frame structure with a boxwood-scented cemetery. Leaving the town of West River, Owensville Road winds mainly downhill past tobacco farms and their weathered gray barns. The vertical slats on the barns slant open to allow air drying of the hanging tobacco leaves.

24.7   Owensville Road crosses Muddy Creek Road (MD 468) and becomes Galesville Road.

On your right just before the intersection is Dixon's Sunoco, a good example of old-time gas station architecture (sodas available). Across the intersection lies the Old Quaker Burying Ground, founded in 1672, which may be explored through a gate in the picket fence. A Quaker meeting house that once stood here burned during the Civil War.

25.5 The Pink Domain Antique Store (left) is chock-full of china, bric-a-brac, and other old things. The owners will be happy to conduct you to another building across the road that holds furniture.

25.6 The West River Market & Deli (left) has groceries and excellent carry-out sandwiches, and the building also houses a gift and antique shop. There are picnic tables in the yard, but you may want to carry your sandwiches down to the waterfront. Next door to the market are two art galleries, and across the road is a marker showing that William Penn passed this way to board a boat across the Chesapeake.

25.7   The road meets the waterfront, where there is a small park.

You may picnic here or try one of Galesville's several restaurants, all of which feature seafood. The Topside Inn is on the left at the intersection of MD 255 and Riverside Drive. A few hundred yards to the right is Steamboat Landing, a restaurant set on pilings in the river. It offers informal outdoor dining and will also arrange boat rides. Turn left on Riverside Drive to Pirates Cove (right), which offers both food and lodging. Just past Pirates Cove, sandwiched between a marina and the West River Sailing Club, stands narrow Elizabeth Dixon Park, which features two picnic tables under a tree by the water. When you finish admiring the view of the West and Rhode Rivers flowing into Chesapeake Bay, read the poem by Elizabeth Dixon that's engraved on a plaque set in a rock. A sampling reads: "Even the sun has a broken path/ As it glistens across the sea./ But the bright spot in the path it seems/ Is always the furthest from me."

Ideally, you should linger awhile in Galesville, boat-watching from the deck of the Steamboat Landing Restaurant as you sip a

Although it's nearly impossible to cart antiques away by bicycle, the Pink Domain in Galesville, Maryland, is well worth a browse.

Bloody Mary with Old Bay seasoning dusted around the rim of the glass. You could dine here on crabs or other local fare, and spend the night—either in the Inn at Pirates Cove (301-261-5050) or at Oakwood, an 1840 manor house that now offers bed and breakfast (301-261-5338). If you must get back to Washington, however, you'll have to cut short your visit to get home before dark. Although alternative routes were explored, none are recommended, so you'll have to reverse direction.

29.1   Turn right on Owensville Sudley Road.

30.4   Turn right on MD 2.

30.6   Turn right on Old Solomons Island Road.

31.1   Old Solomons Island Road ends. Cross MD 2 and enter Harwood Road.

33.5   Turn right on Wayson Road.

34.8   Turn left on Queen Anne Bridge Road.

36.0   Turn right on Patuxent River Road.

36.9   Turn left on MD 214. Watch for traffic.

38.2   Turn right on Queen Anne Bridge Road.

40.3   After you cross US 301, Queen Anne Bridge Road becomes Mitchellville Road. Continue on Mitchellville Road.

41.6   Turn left on Mount Oak Road.

43.2   Turn left on Church Road. Then make an immediate right on Woodmore Road.

46.2   Cross Enterprise Road. Woodmore Road becomes Lottsford Road.

46.9   Turn right on Lottsford Vista Road.

48.1   Turn left on Ardwick Ardmore Road.

51.1   Following the "M" for Metro signs, turn left on Pennsy Drive and cross the bridge.

51.3   Turn left on Corporate Drive.

51.4   Arrive at New Carrollton Metro station.

Bicycle Repair Service
Family Bicycles, 416 Hampton Park Boulevard, Capitol Heights, Maryland, (301-350-0903)
A & M Cycle, 13002 9th Street, Bowie, Maryland (301-262-4343)

20.

Pedaling around Port Tobacco

Location: Charles County, Maryland
Terrain: Rolling hills with some flat stretches
Road conditions: Paved country roads with light traffic
Distance: 12.4 miles
Highlights: The scenic and historic Port Tobacco valley, 18th-century architecture.

The ghost town of Port Tobacco provides a glimpse into Maryland's 18th-century past — when tobacco was king, rivers were roads, and life revolved around gracious plantation homes, many of which are still standing. Founded on the site of an Indian village with a name that sounded like "Potobac" to the first European settlers, the town soon lived up to its name, shipping out hogsheads of tobacco on ships that sailed in and out of the port. The economy, based on slave labor, supported lavish plantations. When the Civil War took away both soldiers and slaves, the area began to decline. Nature also contributed to the town's demise when the river silted up, stranding the old port. A debate over moving the courthouse west to La Plata, which was served by the railroad, was settled in 1891 when the Port Tobacco courthouse "mysteriously" burned down. The arsonists had thoughtfully moved the records outside, and they were later transferred to La Plata, now the county seat.

Although deserted, the town is not gloomy. You can tour the restored courthouse and museum and one of the few remaining houses. You can also inspect St. Ignatius Church and its cemetery, wander the beach along the river, look at the historic manor houses of Rose Hill, from the road, and Habre de Venture, from closer up.

Start your tour at St. Ignatius Roman Catholic Church, Chapel Point, which has a parking lot. To reach the starting point from the Beltway, take MD 5 south to US 301. Take US 301 south through La Plata to the intersection with MD 427 (Chapel Point Road). Turn right on Chapel Point Road to the church.

0.0 From St. Ignatius, continue west on Chapel Point Road, down a short, steep hill, and around a sharp curve.

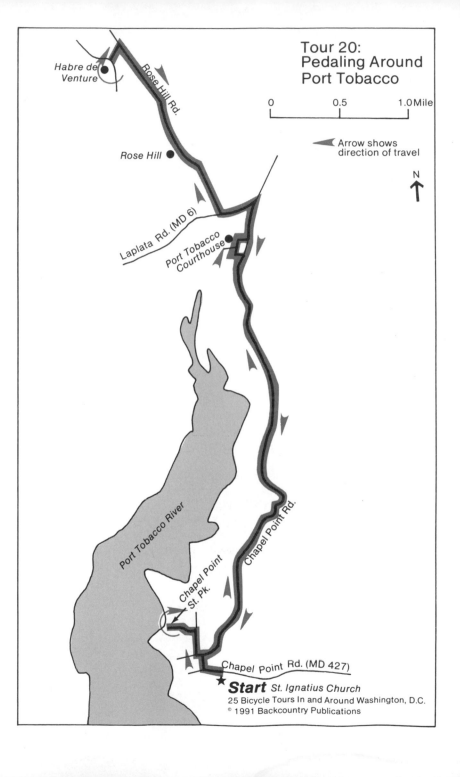

Tour 20:
Pedaling Around
Port Tobacco

Habre de Venture

Rose Hill Rd.

Rose Hill

Laplata Rd. (MD 6)

Port Tobacco Courthouse

0   0.5   1.0 Mile

Arrow shows
direction of travel

N

Port Tobacco River

Chapel Point Rd.

Chapel Point St. Pk.

Chapel Point Rd. (MD 427)

★ **Start** *St. Ignatius Church*
25 Bicycle Tours In and Around Washington, D.C.
© 1991 Backcountry Publications

Rosy-red brick St. Ignatius church was built in 1789 on the site of a chapel built by Father Andrew White, who sailed into Maryland with the first group of settlers in 1634. The adjacent manor house, which dates from 1741, was built on the site of an earlier house. It has been occupied since then by Jesuits, many of whom are buried in the adjacent graveyard. The graveyard, which slopes down toward the river, is a peaceful place that affords an unsurpassed view of the river, the lush countryside, and, on a hill up the river, Rose Hill, once the home one of George Washington's doctors.

0.5   Take a left at the sign into Chapel Point State Park. The road will curve right, then left to the river, a parking lot, and a pebbly beach.
The sign says "No Swimming" but fishing is allowed and you can wander along the beach and at least wade. Past the duck blind to your left there's a shady picnic site.

0.9   Turn left at the park exit onto Chapel Point Road.
This slightly rolling road leads past tobacco farms, woods, and a few suburban-type dwellings.

4.8   At the historical marker, turn left into the old courthouse square.
Most of the homes around the square, with 18th-century dates on them, are privately owned and inhabited. After securing your bike, however, you can visit the restored courthouse and museum for a nominal fee. It's open June through August, Wednesday through Sunday 12 to 4 p.m., and April, May, and September through December, weekends 12 to 4 p.m. The museum contains a mock-up of the large settlement, including hotels and tobacco warehouses that once thrived here, as well as gleanings from an archeological dig. You'll find one whimsical exhibit: broken-off clay pipestems. It seems that hotel guests, after smoking, would break off the mouthpiece, leaving a germ-free pipe for the next guest. The entrance fee also covers a 30-minute video and a visit to the "catslide" house, built in 1700 and named for its steep roof. Tobacco grows in a neighboring plot. There is also a picnic table and a well of fresh water for filling water bottles.
After your visit, return to Chapel Point Road and turn left.

5.2   Turn left onto MD 6.
At the intersection with MD 6 stands Murphy's store (left), offering liquor and groceries. You can sit at picnic tables outside the store and order barbecued ribs cooked in a pit on the grounds.

5.5   Turn right onto Rose Hill Road, which climbs a steep hill.

6.2   Take a left on the dirt road (driveway) to Habre de Venture. The road is unmarked but is across Rose Hill Road from an antique shop.

The old courthouse in Port Tobacco, Maryland, once a bustling port and county seat, houses a museum.

As we went to press, Habre de Venture was under restoration by the National Park Service. By the time you read this, the house will probably be ready for visiting. If not, look at it from the road. Built by Thomas Stone, a signer of the Declaration of Independence, the house is strange, almost unique. Its hip-roofed central building and two wings form a crescent. Stone is buried on the grounds — you can see his grave from the dirt road that leads to the house.

After your visit or look, reverse direction, backtracking down Rose Hill Road.

6.9 Turn left onto MD 6.

7.2 Turn right onto Chapel Point Road.

12.3 Follow Chapel Point road around a sharp, uphill curve.

12.4 Return to St. Ignatius.

Bicycle Repair Service
Clinton Bicycle, 8935 Woodyard Road, Clinton, Maryland, (301-868-0033)

21.

Biking to the Beach that Was

Location: Calvert County, Maryland
Terrain: Moderately hilly
Road conditions: Paved roads, one with moderately heavy traffic but with a shoulder.
Distance: 21.2 miles
Highlights: Chesapeake Beach Railway Museum, Rod N Reel Restaurant, North Beach.

Back before there were two cars in every garage, people took the train to the beach. Capitalizing on that fact, a short-line railroad builder from Colorado named Otto Mears designed a resort town on the shores of Chesapeake Bay. And to carry customers to the hotels, race track, casino, bathhouses, boardwalk, and beaches, he built a railroad, which first chugged into Chesapeake Beach station on June 9, 1900. For 35 years the train, nicknamed the Honeysuckle Express, carried passengers and freight from Seat Pleasant near the District line to the beach. It was finally done in by hurricanes, the Great Depression, and the automobile. Although the town is now enjoying a revival, all that's left from its heydey is the railroad station, which has been preserved and turned into the Chesapeake Beach Railway Museum.

This tour follows part of the route of the Honeysuckle Express to the old station, includes a visit to the museum and to the Rod N Reel restaurant next door, and takes you on a ride along neighboring North Beach. The route then loops up through this old bayside resort community and heads back to the starting point. The tour starts at a Park-and-Ride lot on MD 4. To get there, head south on MD 4 from the Beltway. When you have passed the exit for Deale, watch for a sign for Chesapeake Beach. Just past the sign, pull into the park-and-ride lot on your right at Lower Pindell Road.

0.0 Exit the parking lot and ride on the shoulder of MD 4 south to the bottom of the hill.

0.7 Cross MD 4 carefully and head left on MD 260.
The road is straight but rises and falls in roller-coaster hills.

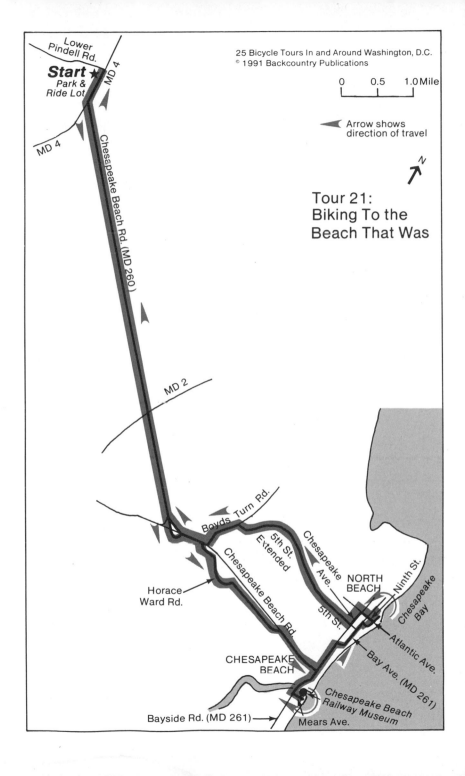

Lower
Pindell Rd.

Start ★
Park &
Ride Lot

MD 4

MD 4

25 Bicycle Tours In and Around Washington, D.C.
© 1991 Backcountry Publications

0   0.5   1.0 Mile

Arrow shows
direction of travel

N

Chesapeake Beach Rd. (MD 260)

Tour 21:
Biking To the
Beach That Was

MD 2

Boyds Turn Rd.

5th St.
Extended

Chesapeake
Ave.

NORTH
BEACH

Ninth St.

Chesapeake
Bay

Horace
Ward Rd.

Chesapeake Beach Rd

5th St.

Atlantic Ave.

CHESAPEAKE
BEACH

Bay Ave. (MD 261)

Bayside Rd. (MD 261)

Chesapeake Beach
Railway Museum

Mears Ave.

4.4   The route crosses MD 2.

4.7 On your right is Owings Antiques, well worth a browsing stop.

6.6   Horace Ward Road goes off to the right in front of a group of stores, including a carry-out food shop. Follow this lovely rural road, which then curves left and parallels the main road.

7.3   Horace Ward Road rejoins MD 260. Turn right on MD 260.

9.0   After a pleasant descent to sea level, turn right on Bayside Road (MD 261).

9.3   Turn left on Mears Avenue to the Chesapeake Beach Railway Museum.

The Museum is open daily May through September from 1 to 4 P.M., and weekends in April and October during the same hours. There is an admission charge. In addition to the restored station house and an old railroad car, there are old photographs and artifacts of the resort's heydey. Adjoining the museum is the Rod N Reel Restaurant, another Chesapeake Beach institution, which dates from 1946. The restaurant specializes in seafood and serves as headquarters for a large head- and charter-boat fleet. The Rod N Reel has a beach and a pier.

After your respite, return to Bayside Road and turn right, heading north along the bay.

10.4   In the town of North Beach, which had fallen from its previous grace and become a down-at-the-heels hangout but which is now undergoing gentrification, MD 261 makes a turn to the right, then turns left and runs along the beach as Bay Avenue.

Antique shops and art galleries are available for browsing.

10.9   Turn right on Atlantic Avenue at the Nice 'N Fleazy antique store for a look at some of the old bayside cottages now being spruced up.

11.0   Turn left on Ninth Street.

11.2   Turn left on Chesapeake Street.

11.5   Turn right on Fifth Street, which runs uphill past the old bungalows and becomes Fifth Street Extended, a country road.

13.7   Turn left on Boyds Turn Road.

14.3   Turn right on Chesapeake Beach Road (MD 260).

20.5   Cross MD 4 and turn right, walking your bike on the shoulder.

21.2   Enter the Park-and-Ride lot.

A sign that once warned trains to slow to a stop tells a cyclist that the Chesapeake Beach Railroad Museum is just ahead.

Bicycle Repair Service
Capital Bicycle Center, 25 Old Solomons Island Road, Annapolis, (410-266-5510)

22.

Trees and Beaches of Calvert County

Location: Calvert County, Maryland
Terrain: Moderately hilly
Road conditions: Paved roads, a few stretches with moderately heavy traffic
Distance: 25.7 miles
Highlights: The American Chestnut Land Trust, Scientists Cliffs on the Chesapeake Bay, Long Beach, the Battle Creek Cypress Swamp and Nature Center, Christ Episcopal Church.

Calvert County, Maryland, is a finger of land between the Chesapeake Bay and the Patuxent River just south of Washington. Its main highway, MD 4, is a southern extension of Washington's Pennsylvania Avenue. Although suburbia is creeping inexorably southward through Calvert, it's still a county where time is marked by the rhythm of the tobacco-growing, oystering, and crabbing seasons.

This tour visits two bayside communities but also takes in two of the county's more unusual attractions: the American Chestnut Land Trust, where dedicated volunteers are trying to revive the blighted and almost extinct American chestnut and where one 80-foot specimen still stands tall, and the Battle Creek Cypress Swamp, a sanctuary for the northernmost stand of the bald cypress.

The trip begins at Christ Episcopal Church in Port Republic. The church, whose present building dates from 1772, is locally famous for the jousting tournament held on the grounds each August. (Jousting is the state sport of Maryland.) To reach the church parking lot from the Washington Beltway, take MD 4 south to the intersection with MD 264 (Broomes Island Road). Turn right on MD 264 and continue .3 miles to the church (left). It's about an hour's drive from Washington.

0.0 Leave the Christ Church parking lot and turn right on MD 264.

0.3 Cross MD 4 very carefully and continue on Old Solomons Island Road (MD 765), which is sometimes marked as St. Leonard Road.

0.8 At the intersection of Parkers Creek Road there's an antique store. Turn left on Parkers Creek Road.

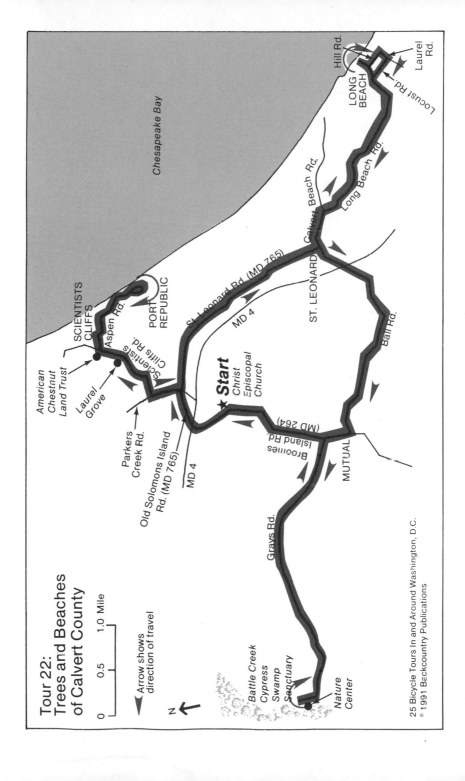

Tour 22:
Trees and Beaches
of Calvert County

Chesapeake Bay

Hill Rd.

Laurel Rd.

LONG BEACH

Locust Rd.

Long Beach Rd.

Calvert Beach Rd.

St. Leonard Rd. (MD 765)

MD 4

ST. LEONARD

Ball Rd.

SCIENTISTS CLIFFS

American Chestnut Land Trust

Aspen Rd.

PORT REPUBLIC

Scientists Cliffs Rd.

Laurel Grove

Parkers Creek Rd.

Old Solomons Island Rd. (MD 765)

MD 4

Start
Christ Episcopal Church

Broomes Island Rd. (MD 264)

MUTUAL

Grays Rd.

Battle Creek Cypress Swamp Sanctuary

Nature Center

25 Bicycle Tours In and Around Washington, D.C.
© 1991 Beckcountry Publications

0   0.5   1.0 Mile

◄— Arrow shows direction of travel

N

Historic Christ Church in Port Republic, Maryland, site of an annual jousting tournament, marks the starting point of a Calvert County tour.

1.1 **Turn right on Scientists' Cliffs Road.**

On your left on this rolling, wooded road is the Jewell Glass Laurel Grove. Dr. Jewell Glass, a mineralogist with the US Geological Survey, died in 1965 and willed this piece of land—steeply sloping and dominated by laurel thickets—to the Nature Conservancy.

2.0 On the left is the main entrance to the American Chestnut Land Trust, where dedicated volunteers—many of them scientists and residents of Scientists Cliffs—are trying to revitalize the American chestnut by breeding it with other strains of chestnut. Lock your bike and follow the hiking trail to one sturdy survivor, an 80-foot chestnut, blighted but unbowed. Take a trail map from the box in the small parking lot.

After your hike, turn right into the entrance to the community of Scientists Cliffs, which was started in the 1930s by a scientist who was the leading expert on the chestnut blight. The community was founded to give hard-working scientists, many of them government employees, a place to commune with nature. Dwellings were required to be rustic and modest. Many of the original cabins are still standing and occupied, and new dwellings are supposed to conform to the spirit of the place. All seem to have well-tended but natural-looking gardens. The community is private, but no one will object if well-behaved cyclists want to bike through. The road, which is named "Aspen," winds to the right past a good example of a Maryland tobacco barn.

2.8   **The road ends at a beach and boat ramp on the Chesapeake Bay.**
To the south, the towering sandstone cliffs of Calvert extend as far as the eye can see.

After a respite here, follow Aspen Road back to the intersection with Scientists' Cliffs Road.

3.6   **Turn left on Scientists' Cliffs Road.**

4.5   **Turn left on Parkers Creek Road.**

4.8   **Turn left on St. Leonard Road (MD 765 or Solomons Island Road).**
This used to be the main road, before a modern MD 4 was completed a few years ago, so it's sort of a ghost highway, with services and businesses that have been by-passed by progress. It's a good biking road with a wide shoulder, and heavy traffic uses MD 4.

7.2 A cluster of buildings on your right marks the small settlement of St. Leonard. Beuhler's Market is highly recommended for picnic supplies and carry-out food. The crab cake and shrimp dinners, with freshly made fries, are especially good.

7.2   **At St. Leonard, turn left on Calvert Beach Road.**

7.7   **Turn right on Long Beach Drive.**

9.8   **Long Beach Drive ends at the beach in the old bungalow colony of Long Beach, where houses built in the 1920s and 1930s nestle in the**

hills that overlook the beach. After a picnic or walk on the beach, turn back on Long Beach Road.

10.0   Turn left on Hill Road, which lives up to its name but affords a tour of this pleasant old resort town.

10.6   Hill Road ends. Turn right on Laurel Road and take the next right turn on Locust Road.

11.0   Turn left on Long Beach Drive.

13.1   Turn left on Calvert Beach Road and continue back through St. Leonard and across MD 4, where Calvert Beach Road becomes Ball Road.

      Ball Road climbs some hills and skirts the rural settlement of Mutual.

16.0   Balls Road ends. Turn right on MD 264 (Broomes Island Road).

16.2   Turn left on Grays Road.

20.4   Turn left into the driveway of the Battle Creek Cypress Swamp Sanctuary.

      The sanctuary and nature center are open April through September, Tuesday through Saturday from 10 a.m. to 5 p.m. and Sunday from 1 to 5 p.m. During the winter months the area closes at 4:30. Admission is free.

      The focal point of the preserve is a nature trail built on a boardwalk over the swamp. The majestic bald cypresses tower as high as a hundred feet overhead and their feathery deciduous needles form a cathedral-like canopy, sheltering many kinds of birds and splashing filtered light on the swamp below. Watch for turtles and frogs among the sleek knobs that poke through the mud. These knobs are the knees of the trees, an extension of the bald cypress root system. They help brace the tree and may provide oxygen to underwater roots. This really is a special place that, in the words of the promotional brochure, "recalls a time some 100,000 years ago when large parts of Maryland were covered with swamps, and saber-toothed tigers and mammoths roamed the landscape."

      After your visit, turn right out of the parking lot onto Grays Road, heading back toward MD 264.

24.6   Grays Road ends. Turn left on MD 264 (Broomes Island Road).

25.7   Turn right into Christ Church parking lot.

Bicycle Repair Service
Cycle 90, MD 4, Solomons, Maryland, (410-326-0283)

23.

St. Mary's Meander

Location: St. Mary's County, Maryland
Terrain: Mainly flat with a few rolling hills
Road conditions: A short distance on a dirt road, then paved roads with light traffic and/or shoulders
Distance: 32.7 miles
Highlights: Historic St. Mary's City, St. Inigoes Church, the Confederate Memorial, Point Lookout State Park, St. Michael's Manor and Vineyard.

St. Mary's County, the first foothold of the Europeans in Maryland, was founded in the early 1600s and has changed relatively little since. St. Mary's City, Maryland's first capital, has been the scene of intense archeological and reconstruction activity in recent years. It's now possible to board a replica of the boat that brought the original settlers, to eat in an "ordinary," or inn, that sheltered travelers, to enter the reconstructed statehouse and to chat with actors who play 17th-century tobacco farmers and their indentured servants. But even after you leave the exhibit areas, the county probably looks much as it did when the first settlers farmed tobacco and fished the nearby waters.

The tour begins at the Chancellor's Point Natural History Area in St. Mary's City. To get there from the Beltway, take MD 5 south to the intersection with MD 235. Follow MD 235 south through the town of Lexington Park. At Mattapany Road, turn right, following the signs for St. Mary's City. At the intersection with MD 5, turn left. Then make an immediate right on Rosecroft Road. Follow Rosecroft Road past the visitors' center to the Chancellor's Point Natural History Area, which has a parking lot, a replica of a woodland Indian long house, and picnic tables in the woods overlooking a beach on the St. Mary's River. Your problem will be leaving this lovely area to do the rest of the tour.

0.0 Exit the parking lot and follow the hard-packed dirt back to Rosecroft Road.

0.3 Turn left on Rosecroft Road, which is paved.

1.0 On your right is the Godiah Spray Tobacco Plantation, a re-

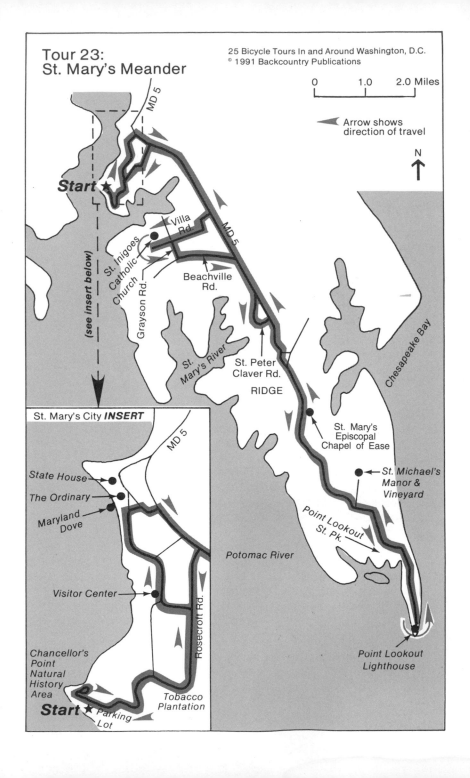

Tour 23:
St. Mary's Meander

25 Bicycle Tours In and Around Washington, D.C.
© 1991 Backcountry Publications

0   1.0   2.0 Miles

Arrow shows
direction of travel

N

MD 5

Start

(see insert below)

St. Inigoes Catholic Church

Villa Rd.

Grayson Rd.

Beachville Rd.

MD 5

St. Mary's River

St. Peter Claver Rd.

RIDGE

St. Mary's Episcopal Chapel of Ease

St. Michael's Manor & Vineyard

Chesapeake Bay

Point Lookout St. Pk.

Potomac River

Point Lookout Lighthouse

St. Mary's City **INSERT**

MD 5

State House

The Ordinary

Maryland Dove

Visitor Center

Rosecroft Rd.

Chancellor's Point Natural History Area

Start ★ Parking Lot

Tobacco Plantation

creation of a 1660s tobacco farm. The Sprays may be cooking up lunch when you arrive and may invite you to join them — if you're willing to pull a few weeds from the garden in return.

1.7 A road to the left leads to the visitors' center, where you may purchase tickets and obtain maps of the historic area.

From here, take the trail that leads to the "ordinary" (tavern), the Maryland Dove, and the reconstructed statehouse and other attractions.

After your visit, exit through the parking lot in back of the ordinary to MD 5 south.

2.6 Turn right on MD 5.

You'll encounter little traffic on MD 5 at this point, and there is a wide shoulder.

4.8 Turn right on Villa Road.

6.4 On your right is St. Inigoes Catholic Church, constructed in 1785 on the site of a church built in 1638 by Jesuits. You can get the key to the church at the gate to the naval air facility next door. Volunteers from this facility helped restore the church, which is surrounded by a cemetery. After your visit, go back to Villa Road and retrace your steps for .4 mile.

6.8 Turn right on Grayson's Road.

7.2 Turn left on Beachville Road, which climbs a hill.

8.5 Turn right on MD 5.

9.4 Turn right on St. Peter Claver Road, a diversion from MD 5. Follow this road through a small village and past a park until it rejoins the main road.

10.2 At the bottom of the hill, turn right on MD 5, which leads through the small settlement of Ridge.

12.2 On your left is St. Mary's Episcopal Chapel of Ease, a pleasant white frame church.

13.0 On your right is Buzzy's Country Store, which sells food, fishing licenses, and gasoline. Just past here, the shoulder ends. Ride carefully on the road.

14.7 On your right is a memorial to 3,384 Confederate prisoners of war who died at a prison camp at nearby Point Lookout. Poet Sidney Lanier was one of the prisoners who survived the extremely harsh and unsanitary conditions at this camp. Just past the memorial, MD 5 turns right into Point Lookout State Park, which offers

Proprietor Joe Dick presses grapes for the wine bottled at St. Michael's Manor near Point Lookout, Maryland.

superb fishing, crabbing, and clamming opportunities as well as a swimming beach and picnic area. There is an admission charge for the swimming area. The road leads over a narrow, sometimes windy causeway between the Chesapeake Bay and the Potomac Rivers, affording spectacular views of the wild, wind-whipped, end-of-the-world landscape. At the point where these two bodies of water come together stands a lighthouse.

17.0 At the lighthouse, which now houses a satellite tracking facility, reverse direction and follow the road out of the park.

20.0 Turn right on a dirt driveway to St. Michael's Manor and Vineyard. The house was built in 1805 on Long Neck Creek and the owners now offer bed and breakfast (301-872-4025). They make red and rosé wines from grapes grown on the estate and sell them in bottles labeled with a drawing of the house.

21.0 After leaving St. Michael's Manor, turn right on MD 5.

30.8 Turn left on Rosecroft Road.

32.7 Arrive at Chancellor's Point Natural History Area.

Bicycle Repair Service
Mike's Bike Shop, 447-C Great Mills Road, Lexington Park, Maryland, (301-863-7887).

24.

Cycling to the Covered Bridges

Location: Frederick County, Maryland
Terrain: Moderately hilly
Road conditions: Paved country roads with little traffic
Distance: 24.6 miles
Highlights: Three covered bridges, Apple's Church, Catoctin Furnace, the
    Cozy Inn.

Covered bridges make perfect sense: since bridge surfaces freeze before solid highways, why not put a roof over them? But modern road
planners don't like covered bridges, and the wooden structures, prey to
the debilitating effects of time and weather as well as to modernization,
are fast disappearing. There were once 52 covered bridges in Maryland.
Only eight remain, and three of them are within easy cycling distance of
the pleasant town of Thurmont, north of Frederick.

In June, 1991, one of Frederick County's historic bridges, the Loy's
Station Bridge, became a victim of insurance fraud: the owner of a pickup
truck decided to burn it on the bridge and ended up burning the bridge,
too. A few months after the fire, the Roddy Road Bridge was closed after a
truck rammed into it. Both bridges should be repaired by summer 1993.

Detours around both bridges are provided, in case the completion is
delayed until after you make this trip. To check the status of the work, call
Al Hudac at 301-696-2928.

Start in the parking lot of the Cozy Inn in Thurmont. To get there,
take I-270 north from the Beltway to Frederick. At Frederick, I-270 runs
into US 15. Take US 15 north to the Thurmont exit and follow signs to the
Cozy Inn. Tell the clerk you'll be back in about four hours, and come
back hungry. The all-you-can-eat buffet is not for the faint of heart.

0.0   Exit the parking lot and turn left on Frederick Road.

0.3   Just past the community park, turn left on Church Street.
           You are now in the heart of Thurmont, founded in 1751 by a
           westward-bound family who stopped here with a sick child. They
           stayed on, started a forge, and other industries grew up to serve the
           surrounding farms.

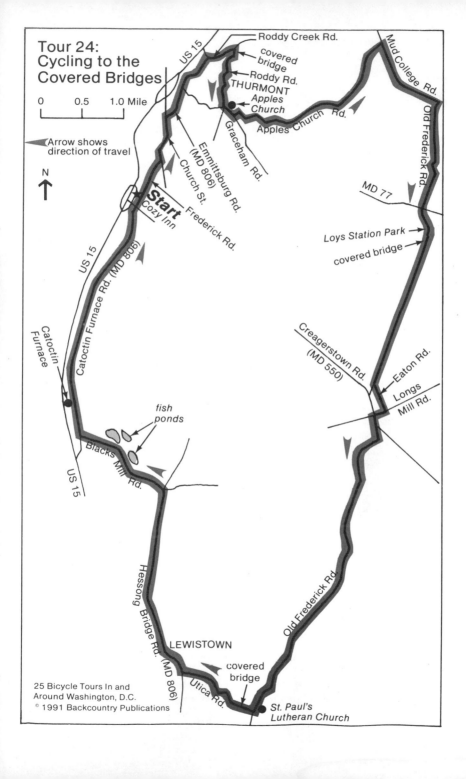

Tour 24:
Cycling to the
Covered Bridges

0   0.5   1.0 Mile

Arrow shows direction of travel

N

Roddy Creek Rd.

covered bridge

Roddy Rd.

US 15

THURMONT

Apples Church

Mud College Rd.

Old Frederick Rd.

Emmittsburg Rd. (MD 806)

Church St.

Graceham Rd.

Apples Church Rd.

MD 77

Start
Cozy Inn

Frederick Rd.

Loys Station Park

covered bridge

US 15

Catoctin Furnace Rd. (MD 806)

Catoctin Furnace

Creagerstown Rd. (MD 550)

Eaton Rd.

Longs Mill Rd.

fish ponds

Blacks Mill Rd.

US 15

Old Frederick Rd.

Hessong Bridge Rd. (MD 806)

LEWISTOWN

covered bridge

25 Bicycle Tours In and
Around Washington, D.C.
© 1991 Backcountry Publications

Utica Rd.

St. Paul's
Lutheran Church

Cyclists pause to read the history of the covered bridge across Owens Creek near Thurmont, Maryland.

0.9 Turn right on Emmitsburg Road (MD 806), which passes a horse farm and then travels through a small industrial area.

Detour #1

1.4 *Turn right on Eyler Road.*

1.9 *At the intersection with Roddy Road, Eyler Road becomes Graceham Road.*

2.0 *Bear left on Apples Church Road and continue the regular tour. This detour reduces the total distance by 1.2 miles, so you may want to substract that number from each mileage point.*

1.9 Turn right on Roddy Creek Road, which follows Owens Creek through a pleasant wooded area.

> 2.4 The first and smallest of the three covered bridges, a picturesque barn red, carries you over Owens Creek. This is a good spot for wading, and the horses in the neighboring field will probably come up to the fence to pose for pictures.

2.4 After crossing the creek, make a sharp right onto Roddy Road, which takes you over rolling hills and past small farms.

3.2 At the intersection with Graceham Road, bear left. Then make the next left onto Apples Church Road.

> The stone church (left) that gives the road its name dates from 1826 and was built to serve the German community.

6.1 Make a sharp right on Mud College Road.

> This is a rural road that winds around to the left and has a short gravel stretch.

7.4 Turn right on Old Frederick Road.

8.8 Old Frederick Road crosses MD 77. If you see a sign indicating that the bridge is out, use Detour #2. Otherwise, continue south on Old Frederick Road.

Detour #2

9.9 *Turn right on Old Mill Road, a hard-packed gravel road that winds down a hill, crosses Owens Creek and returns to Old Frederick Road beyond the Loy's Station Bridge.*

11.5 *Turn left on Old Frederick Road and rejoin the main tour. You have added 2.5 miles to the total distance you will travel, so add that number to each mileage point given for the rest of the trip.*

> 9.1 At Loys Station Park, Old Frederick Road bears right, taking you over the second covered bridge, which is also made of red, beveled German clapboard and also crosses Owens Creek. There's a swimming hole under the bridge, and just downstream the creek flows

over some minirapids. This is an ideal picnic spot, with picnic tables but no changing facilities other than a portable toilet. After the park, Old Frederick Road climbs a hill. At the top you'll see a spectacular view of the Catoctins. A little farther on there's a duck pond.

11.2 Turn left on Eaton Road.

11.6 Turn right on Longs Mill Road and proceed to the intersection with Creagarstown Road (MD 550). Turn left.
There's a small food store just after the intersection.

11.9 Turn right on Old Frederick Road, which cuts across some suburban developments.

16.1 St. Paul's Lutheran Church is on a hill to your left. Just past the church, turn right on Utica Road.

16.4 Another red covered bridge carries Utica Road over Fishing Creek. The road then winds uphill and down.

17.1 Utica Road ends. Turn right on Hessong Bridge Road.

18.1 Martin's Grocery, in the village of Lewistown, is on your left.

20.0 Turn left on Blacks Mill Road, which skirts Little Hunting Creek.
The stream, which invites wading, is on your left. On your right are fish hatchery ponds, but there is no access to them from this road.

21.3 Turn right on Catoctin Furnace Road (MD 806).

21.8 The ruins on your left are the remains of Catoctin Furnace, which goes back to 1774. The shells used by the Continental Army at the battle of Yorktown were made here. The surrounding park has picnic tables. After you pass the furnace, Catoctin Furnace Road veers close to US 15, becoming a frontage road.

22.4 The Ice Cream Safari serves homemade pie and hot dogs as well as ice cream. Just past the store, Catoctin Furnace Road veers away from the highway again.

23.6 The Blue Mountain Inn (right) is locally famous for its crabs. After passing the inn, the road descends on Thurmont, running a gamut of fast-food restaurants. Watch for traffic where Catoctin Furnace Road joins Frederick Road.

24.6 Turn left into the Cozy Inn.

Bicycle Repair Service
Frederick Bicycles, 1216 West Patrick Street, Frederick, Maryland, (301-663-4452)

A Three-State Tour

25.

Over the River and through the Hills to Harpers Ferry

Location: Maryland, Virginia, and West Virginia
Terrain: Some steep climbs the first day, then rolling or flat
Road conditions: Long stretches on dedicated bike trails, one paved, one unpaved; two short stretches on heavily traveled highways; otherwise, lightly traveled roads
Distance: 71.8 miles
Highlights: Historic Leesburg and Harpers Ferry, the Blue Ridge Mountains and foothills, the Chesapeake and Ohio Canal.

This trip is ideal for a three-day weekend, although hardy pedalers could easily do it in two days. It involves overnight stays at two youth hostels. The Bear's Den hostel at Bluemont, a 1930s castle that was the summer home of opera singer Francesca Caspar Lawson, sits astride the Blue Ridge, a stone's throw from the Appalachian Trail. The comfortable, well-organized Harpers Ferry hostel is actually on the Maryland shore beside the C & O Canal and an easy walk or ride to the historic area. Reservations should be made well in advance if you plan to use either of these hostels; they are popular with groups. Call 703-554-8708 for reservations at Bluemont and 301-834-7652 for reservations at the Harpers Ferry hostel.

Day 1: Whites Ferry to Bear's Den Hostel

The trip begins with a boat ride across the Potomac on historic Whites Ferry. As you wait at the ferry slip, you'll be able to see the General Jubal Early sliding across on its cable. The ferry boat bears the name of a daring Confederate officer who crossed the river hereabouts on his way to raid Washington in 1864. Jubal Early's raid didn't succeed, but it scared the daylights out of Washingtonians because it brought the war right into the city—to Fort Stevens. History doesn't record where Early recrossed the river on his hasty retreat back to Virginia, but pretend it was here. Climb on your metal steed and board the boat that is his

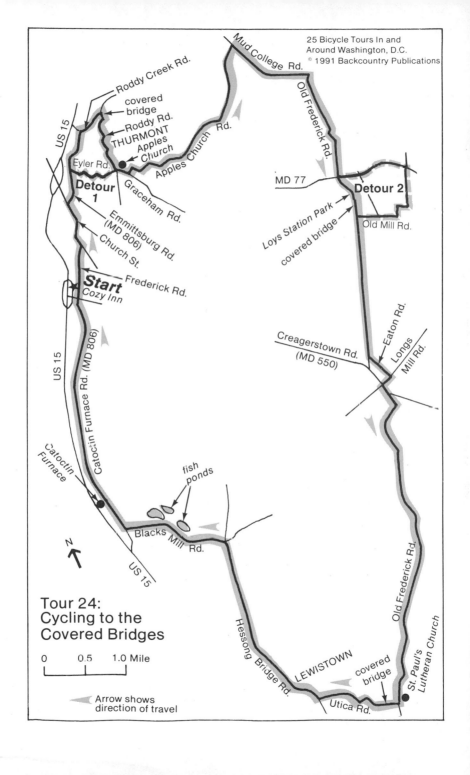

25 Bicycle Tours In and
Around Washington, D.C.
© 1991 Backcountry Publications

Roddy Creek Rd.

covered
bridge

Roddy Rd.

THURMONT

Apples
Church

US 15

Eyler Rd.

Apples Church Rd.

Mud College Rd.

Old Frederick Rd.

MD 77

Detour 2

Loys Station Park

covered bridge

Old Mill Rd.

Detour 1

Graceham Rd.

Emmittsburg Rd.
(MD 806)

Church St.

Start

Cozy Inn

Frederick Rd.

US 15

Catoctin Furnace Rd. (MD 806)

Creagerstown Rd.
(MD 550)

Eaton Rd.

Longs Mill Rd.

Catoctin
Furnace

fish
ponds

Blacks Mill Rd.

US 15

N

Hessong Bridge Rd.

LEWISTOWN

Old Frederick Rd.

St. Paul's Lutheran Church

covered
bridge

Utica Rd.

Tour 24:
Cycling to the
Covered Bridges

0   0.5   1.0 Mile

Arrow shows
direction of travel

namesake, paying 50 cents for the short glide into the former Confederacy. You won't be there, incidentally, until you debark on the other side, for, under the original grant from the King of England, the entire Potomac belongs to Maryland.

To reach Whites Ferry from the Beltway, take I-270 north to the MD 28 exit. Head in the direction of Darnestown and continue to Dawsonville where you will turn left into Whites Ferry Road, MD 107. The ferry is at the end of MD 107. It has a large parking lot and a store for stocking up on picnic supplies. The ferry runs seven days a week, all year around, beginning at 5 a.m. In spring, summer, and fall, it runs until 11 p.m. In winter it stops at 8 p.m. During unusually high water on the Potomac, the ferry may not be able to cross. For information call 301-349-5200.

0.0 **Ride off the ferry on the Virginia side and follow the feeder road up a hill, through woods and rolling farmland to the junction with US 15.**

1.2 **Walk your bike across US 15 and turn left (south). Proceed with caution, preferably on the shoulder of this heavily traveled road.**

Although some maps may lead you to believe you can avoid this road by cutting through Morven Park, you can't—not without hopping fences, trudging through fields, and trespassing on horse pastures. So the only recourse is to tough it out on US 15. The bad part only lasts for two miles.

3.2 **Keep to your right, following US 15 "Business" rather than US 15 "Bypass."**

At the point where the road divides, look on your right for a historic marker commemorating the Civil War Battle of Ball's Bluff. You are now entering Leesburg, founded in 1757 as Georgetown and later renamed to honor Francis Lightfoot Lee, a signer of the Declaration of Independence. Continue down US 15 Business, or King Street. Stock up on picnic supplies; you won't find another store or restaurant for 10 miles.

4.4 **Take a right on W & OD Trail.**

The trail follows the old roadbed of the Washington and Old Dominion Railroad, whose trains ran here from 1859 to 1968. Passengers affectionately called the line "the Virginia creeper," and the term lives on as a popular nickname for the trail. You're sharing the trail with strollers, hikers, and horses. In many places there are unpaved equestrian side trails. Watch out for horse piles.

8.6 **You have now climbed to the highest point on the trail, Clarks Gap. Pass under a century-old stone arch.**

8.8 The trail jogs right, then left, crossing a heavily traveled highway. Follow the trail signs.

> 9.3 At the 39-mile marker you may want to exit the trail via Highland Avenue for a tour of Paeonian Springs, an old, strictly residential town that includes the Museum of the American Workhorse.

> 11.3 The defunct Hamilton Railroad Station stands on your right. Washingtonians once disembarked here to vacation in the boarding houses of this pre–Civil War Quaker settlement.

13.3 The trail seems to end abruptly here, but actually it turns left, crosses the VA 7 by-pass, then leads you into Purcellville. Follow the trail signs.

14.8 The trail ends at the Purcellville railroad station. Turn left on VA 690 and continue .2 miles to Main Street, VA 7. From here you must continue west on VA 7.

> George's Plaza Restaurant, across Main Street, is a good stop for a hearty, inexpensive meal, with excellent milkshakes. Save room for dessert ahead, however. In the towns, riding on the sidewalks is suggested, with due consideration for the rare pedestrian.

> 15.8 The Purcellville Inn, fancier than George's, is on your left. It also offers lodging.

> 18.0 In the village of Round Hill, the Round Hill Diner is on your right. Sidewalks are available.

> 19.2 You'll be glad when you reach High Hill Orchards (right) not only for the food that awaits you but also because, after the sidewalk ends, VA 7 begins to get unpleasant. Buy a pie, some cider, and some apples and relax at one of the picnic tables by the duck pond.

21.7 At the top of a long, steep climb on VA 7, you'll see a sign on the left side of the road marking VA 760 to the pretty hamlet of Bluemont. If you need supplies or just want to see Bluemont, walk your bike across the highway and proceed down 760 to the intersection with VA 734 (.3 miles). Stock up at the picturesque Snickersville General Store at the intersection; then turn right up VA 734 to the intersection with VA 7 (.5 miles).

> This is a steep climb, so if you don't need supplies you may want to skip this side trip. It is, however, your last chance to buy food to cook at the hostel.

22.6 Turn left on VA 601.

> You are now at Snickers Gap, on top of the Blue Ridge, but must climb at bit more to reach the hostel.

The old railroad station in Purcellville, Virginia, marks the western terminus of the Washington and Old Dominion trail.

23.0   Turn on the gravel driveway marked by the hostel sign.

23.4   You have reached the Bear's Den Hostel, elevation 1,300 feet.
When you've checked in and rested a bit, walk down a path to the Appalachian Trail and a spectacular lookout. Stay for sunset.

Day 2: Bear's Den Hostel to Harpers Ferry

23.8   Exit the hostel driveway and turn left on VA 601. Start to brake your downhill ride before you get to VA 7.

24.2   Take a right on VA 7 east.

25.5   Walk your bike across the highway and turn left onto VA 711.
This is a beautiful country road with almost no automobile traffic and lots of old stone houses, orchards, horses, cattle, and rabbits. It's hard-packed dirt and gravel.

26.8 Blackthorne, on the right, dates from 1740, about the time this area, sometimes called "Little Scotland" or "The Land Between the Hills," was settled by Scots.

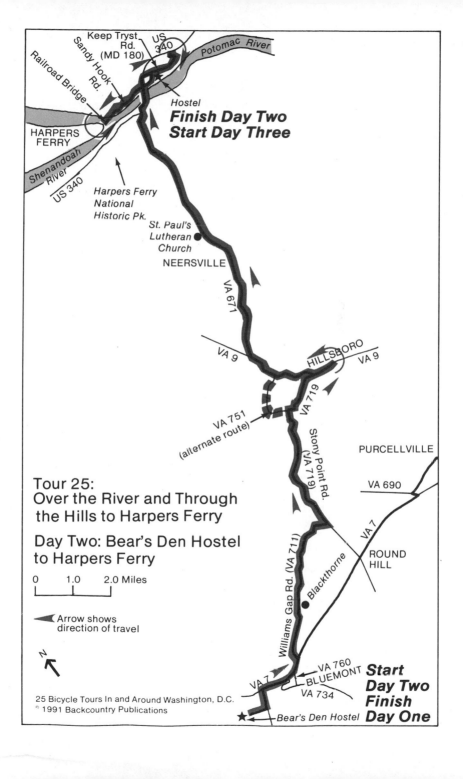

Keep Tryst Rd. (MD 180)

US 340

Potomac River

Sandy Hook Rd.

Railroad Bridge

HARPERS FERRY

Shenandoah River

US 340

Hostel
***Finish Day Two
Start Day Three***

Harpers Ferry National Historic Pk.

St. Paul's Lutheran Church

NEERSVILLE

VA 671

VA 9

HILLSBORO

VA 9

VA 719

VA 751 (alternate route)

Stony Point Rd. (VA 719)

PURCELLVILLE

VA 690

VA 7

ROUND HILL

Williams Gap Rd. (VA 711)

Blackthorne

Tour 25:
Over the River and Through the Hills to Harpers Ferry

Day Two: Bear's Den Hostel to Harpers Ferry

0   1.0   2.0 Miles

◄ Arrow shows direction of travel

N

VA 760
BLUEMONT
VA 734

VA 7

★ ← Bear's Den Hostel

***Start
Day Two
Finish
Day One***

25 Bicycle Tours In and Around Washington, D.C.
© 1991 Backcountry Publications

29.7 Turn left on VA 719, which is paved and sometimes busy.

33.2 VA 719 turns right at the T. Follow this to go into Hillsboro for food or antiques. (If you don't want to see Hillsboro, a lovely ante-bellum town, bear left on VA 751 at the T and rejoin the tour on VA 9.) VA 719 will take you past the ruins of a stone house.

34.5 From 719, turn right on VA 9 into Hillsboro.

There are at least two bed and breakfast inns here, Hillsboro House Bed and Breakfast and The Inn Between the Hills. The well-stocked market at the Exxon station has sandwiches, coffee, sodas, ice cream, and more. An antique store just across the road makes interesting browsing.

After your stop, reverse direction, heading west on VA 9.

36.5 On your left is Lynfield Farm, a picture-book, white-fenced horse farm that welcomes visitors from 9 a.m. to 5 p.m. daily, except Tuesdays. There's no formal tour, but you're free to wander through the stables and watch the hunters and jumpers being put through their paces.

37.1 Take a right on VA 671 at Lineberry's Store.

40.2 The Neersville Store (left), which dates from 1820, sells an eclectic collection of antiques.

40.9 St. Paul's Lutheran Church (left), a stone building dating from 1835, has an inviting graveyard.

44.7 At the intersection with US 340, go left to go into Harpers Ferry, or right to go to the youth hostel, which is on the Maryland side of the Potomac. For the hostel, follow US 340 across the bridge, walking your bike on the narrow sidewalk.

45.1 Turn right on Keep Tryst Road, which is not marked at this point but is the first right turn you can make on the Maryland side of the river.

45.3 Go right on Sandy Hook Road and down the hill to the hostel sign. To tour historic Harpers Ferry, continue down Sandy Hook Road which turns right and runs parallel to the river.

47.2 On your left is a railroad bridge into Harpers Ferry. Carry your bike up the stairs and walk it across the bridge on the pedestrian walkway to the town of Harpers Ferry, much of which is a national historical park.

The town's moment in history came on October 16, 1859, when a small band of abolitionists led by zealot John Brown captured the federal arsenal. The U.S. government sent the Marines under Colonel Robert E. Lee to recapture it in a bloody battle. During the Civil

War the town was captured by General Stonewall Jackson, but only after Union forces had destroyed the arsenal. Lock your bike up here and head for the Visitors' Center for a film orientation and map for a self-guided tour. For a refreshing dip in warm weather, continue from the Visitors' Center down Shenandoah Street to the beach that lines the river.

Reverse direction to return to the hostel.

Day 3: Harpers Ferry to Whites Ferry

50.2 Take a right out of the hostel driveway to the top of Sandy Hook Road.

50.4 Go left on Keep Tryst Road to the Cindy Dee Restaurant for a hearty, trucker-type breakfast. Then backtrack a few hundred yards on Keep Tryst Road, past Sandy Hook Road, and continue down Keep Tryst Road.

51.6 Cross railroad tracks on a path on the right side of the road and enter the C & O Canal towpath. Turn left on the towpath.

The Chesapeake and Ohio Canal, completed in 1850 at a total cost of $11 million, helped transport flour, grain, building stone, whiskey, and coal between Cumberland, Maryland and Georgetown. The mules who pulled the boats walked the towpath, now a 184-mile hiker-biker trail. The trail is hard-packed dirt and can be muddy in wet weather. Call 301-739-4200 for trail conditions.

54.8 Cross under the highway bridge to Virginia.

The town of Brunswick, Maryland, with its busy railroad yards, looms on your left. You'll find a camping area and some picnic tables at Lift Lock #30.

56.5 Cross Catoctin Creek on Catoctin Aqueduct, a three-arch stone crossing trussed by cables.

58.1 Lander Lock House was once home for the tender of Lift Lock #29. Its six-foot lift was the smallest on the canal.

58.7 The pump at the campsite provides an opportunity to fill water bottles.

60.9 Just past Lock #28, you'll see the town of Point of Rocks on your left. This is a good place to buy food and to see the landmark Queen Anne–style railroad station.

62.8 You have reached Nolands Ferry picnic area, which has grills.

65.2 Cross the Monocacy River on Monocacy Aqueduct, a 516-foot span consisting of seven granite arches.

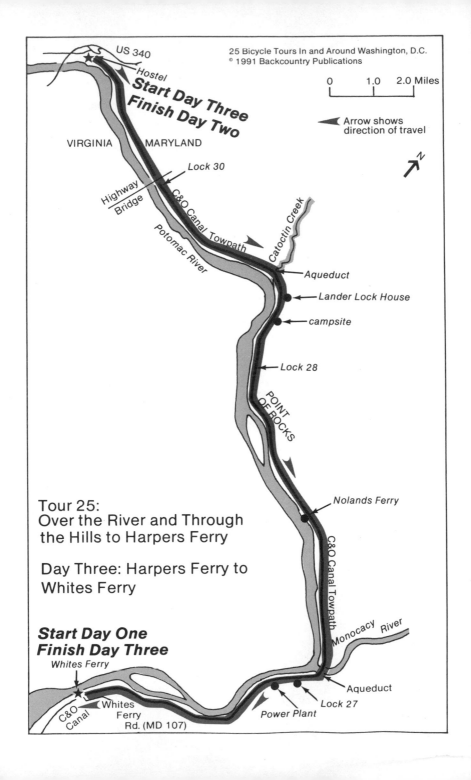

25 Bicycle Tours In and Around Washington, D.C.
© 1991 Backcountry Publications

0   1.0   2.0 Miles

◄ Arrow shows
direction of travel

N

US 340

Hostel

Start Day Three
Finish Day Two

VIRGINIA   MARYLAND

Lock 30

Highway
Bridge

C&O Canal Towpath

Potomac River

Catoctin Creek

Aqueduct

Lander Lock House

campsite

Lock 28

POINT
OF
ROCKS

Nolands Ferry

C&O Canal Towpath

Tour 25:
Over the River and Through
the Hills to Harpers Ferry

Day Three: Harpers Ferry to
Whites Ferry

Start Day One
Finish Day Three

Whites Ferry

C&O Canal

Whites
Ferry
Rd. (MD 107)

Power Plant

Monocacy River

Aqueduct

Lock 27

A cyclist awaits the arrival of the General Jubal Early at White's Ferry, Maryland.

You'll have to walk your bike because the aqueduct, completed in 1833, is now held together by a steel support structure that must be climbed over. A pleasant park surrounds the area where the Monocacy runs into the Potomac.

65.9 A footbridge leads to the lockhouse for Lift Lock #27.

66.6 Pass an electric power generating plant on your left.

71.8 MD 107 crosses the towpath. Turn right to the Whites Ferry parking lot.

Bicycle Repair Service

Bicycle Outfitters, 19 Catoctin Circle NE, Leesburg, Virginia, (703-777-6126)
Frederick Bicycles, 1216 West Patrick Street, Frederick, Maryland,
(301-663-4452)

Also from The Countryman Press and Backcountry Publications

The Countryman Press and Backcountry Publications, long known for fine books on travel and outdoor recreation, offer a range of practical and readable manuals.

Bicycling

Keep on Pedaling: The Complete Guide to Adult Bicycling,
    by Norman D. Ford, $12.95

Bicycle Touring Guides

25 Bicycle Tours on Delmarva, $10.00
25 Bicycle Tours in Eastern Pennsylvania, $8.95
20 Bicycle Tours in the Finger Lakes, $10.00
20 Bicycle Tours in the Five Boroughs (NYC), $8.95
25 Bicycle Tours in the Hudson Valley, $10.00
25 Bicycle Tours in Maine, $10.00
30 Bicycle Tours in New Hampshire, $11.00
25 Bicycle Tours in New Jersey, $10.00
20 Bicycle Tours in and around New York City, $9.00
25 Bicycle Tours in Ohio's Western Reserve, $11.95
25 Bicycle Tours in Vermont, $9.95
25 Mountain Bike Tours in Massachusetts: From the Connecticut River
    to the Atlantic, $9.95
25 Mountain Bike Tours in Vermont, $9.95

Other Books for Washington area residents and visitors:

Fifty Hikes in Eastern Pennsylvania, $12.00
Fifty Hikes in Central Pennsylvania, $10.95
Pennsylvania Trout Streams and Their Hatches, $14.95
Virginia Trout Streams, $15.00
Walks and Rambles on the Delmarva Peninsula, $10.95

We offer many more books on hiking, walking, fishing, and canoeing, in New England, New York State, the Mid-Atlantic states, and the Midwest—plus books on travel, nature, and many other subjects.

Our titles are available in bookshops and in many sporting goods stores, or they may be ordered directly from the publisher. When ordering by mail, please add $2.50 per order for shipping and handling. To order or obtain a complete catalog, please write The Countryman Press, Inc., P.O. Box 175, Woodstock, VT 05091.